Dedication:

I dedicate this book to all the people who thirst for more knowledge about the Word of God and the lives He gave testimony in scripture. May we, as readers, be inspired to seek Him first in all we do.

*"As you come to Him, a living stone rejected by men,
but in the sight of God; chosen and precious.
You yourselves, like living stones, are being built up as a spiritual
house, to be a Holy Priesthood, to offer spiritual sacrifices acceptable To
God through Jesus Christ."*

1 Peter 2:4-5

Introduction:

No distinguished leader wakes up one day and decides to become great among his peers. He doesn't set out to make millions in his lifetime. He doesn't look into the mirror and see a legend. He sees a young boy striving for purpose in a world so vast that he can't fathom making a mark on it. When we read about how great men have left their mark on the world, we only see the end of their story. We see what they want us to see. We see what they want us to take away from their pain. We see something in the end, so powerful, that he makes us want to be like him.

What we don't see are the struggles that man had to overcome to become great. Sure, he had to overcome poverty, but how did he do it? We see that he has overcome hunger, but how did he do it? We are told he couldn't believe in himself and that he struggled with fear, but how did he overcome it? Their stories have always left me with more questions than answers. That was until God showed me the recipe for greatness. There is a way, a hard way, through it, but it is worth it. If you can listen, you too can become great!

~2 Timothy 2:15~

Table of Contents:

Chapter One: Self-Doubt

1

Everyone begins their story differently. Some babies were given wealth, some poverty. Some babies had good parents; some did not. Some children had a mentor to teach them about everything they would need to know in life at home; some only had what they could observe. But one day in each of our lives, one realization hits us all. We are not enough. We do not have the same strengths, money, power, or fame to do what we want to get done in this world. We can read biographies, testimonies, and Wikipedia pages till we are consumed with a jealous rage, or like most of us, we can set out on our journey to discover our path to becoming great.

I don't know about your path, but in my experience, I always fell short of doing anything worthy of attention. Sure, I helped others. I was a nice person. I worked hard and obtained many belongings, but never enough to be called great in anyone else's book. I felt like a blip in someone else's tale. I never felt I had the control over my life to do something worthy of attention and, therefore, could not lead others anywhere. So, when I would look at other's achievements, I would always fall short, and deep down inside my heart I would never live my life as if I had the power to make anything happen. I thought I would die living that lie to its fullest.

So how do others do it? Are they dealt a source of power or strength that God forgot to give me? Why did He give them power, wealth, and fame but then leave me to be a nobody? Why didn't my parents have the glory and riches that they could've left me with to help with my college tuition? Or why couldn't God have given me a life that I could easily testify about and overcome some obstacle to give my life a great testimony? Why wasn't I made of more? Why couldn't I have more? Why couldn't I do more?

I have struggled with these questions for most of my life. I won't lie to you; my life is so plain I think there is a bland color in the Crayola Box with my name on it. Right between Plain Jane and John Smith. I look at the spelling of my name, and I tell people that I didn't know what my parents were smoking when they made me! Although in my mind, I saw my life as a miracle, I never felt good enough for anything or anyone. But somewhere deep inside my soul, I thought I had something that could benefit humanity. Because of my family and my choices in love, I was encouraged to believe the opposite of what I felt. That I was a nobody and no one would ever miss me if I was gone. That the lie I felt in my soul was just that, a lie.

It was after my divorce from my first husband that God intervened and told me a different story. It was a long journey. If you would like to know more, please read my first book, <u>My Beloved.</u> There, you will read about how God showed me that to Him, I was everything. That I was worthy of His Love and that was all that mattered. It's not a long book. If I remember correctly, I don't think it broke 80,000 words, but it is a portion of my journey that God brought me out of a bad marriage and a horrible custody dispute to put my feet back on solid ground with Him. He began to speak to me as His own. He interceded on my behalf to restore what the enemy had taken from me. God gave me hope, love, strength, and peace, but most of all, He gave me back my ability to believe in myself again.

Like I said, I was never the one who thought my life would include walking on a red carpet or being given an achievement award. But in my youth, I had hope that tomorrow would bring success. At that time, a wonderful and successful husband, a home, a family, and a white picket fence with a pot roast in the oven was a piece of Heaven that I could obtain. But as my youth faded, I began waiting longer and later for my husband to come home for dinner. Only to realize that my version of Heaven was fleeting, as was he. The family I once loved and called my own became my worst enemy. Friends turned into foes. Community and justice were a disappointment. No one was there for me but God, my mother, and my grandmother.

No one could take God from me, and that loyalty was tested in court. They tried to prove I was crazy and heard voices because I heard the Lord speak. They tried to diminish my abilities as a mother because I was faithful to my God. I stood by Him, and He took from me the rage and anger that should have been there. I was labeled unsound because I did not get outraged like any other normal mother who had this level of attack committed against her. They said anger and rage would be understandable to anyone who knew what I had been faced with. They said I had to go to these psychologists, and they would see if this was just an act. They said to take these health and mental examinations to see if there was something wrong with me because there was no way that I could maintain this act much longer. They said that I could not deny the pain and hurt its rightful place in my emotions, but to be honest, they were not in me. I did not have them because I had given them to God when I surrendered my life to Him. When I learned my life was no longer mine but His to do His Will. He told me in the scriptures that if I listened to Him, then He would give me the desires of my heart. I had to jump through more hoops than any custody dispute case has ever been put through, and they still couldn't find a reason for my peace. But in my heart and mind, I knew where my peace came from. It came from my God.

Even as I type this reflection into my past, the sting of those fiery arrows still hurts. My journey was marked by the enemy, and it used every arrow in its arsenal that it could. There were boxes of tries in the courts, but tens of thousands of arrows were laid at my left and right. The fiery arrows the enemy used to have me taken out. Even some that should have made me want to take myself out. Nothing hurts worse than to have someone who should love you unconditionally, like a relative, come against you by not wanting you in their life because another's lies might be true. However, it was nothing compared to the attacks on my mind that were happening. I was drowning in the debris of a life that I was trying to hold onto. My husband, my daughter, my home, car, boat, rental homes, and businesses were all gone in one man's selfish desires. There was nothing that I could do about it. It was gone. In the very beginning, when he first walked out the door, I sat on the floor of the living room on my hands and knees, crying out to God. "Why did you let this happen to me? God, why is this happening to me?" and yes, believe it or not, He answered me right away.

I had just laid my daughter down for the night, and as I

cried, His Voice pierced the darkness and sadness that was upon me and said something that changed my life. He said, "This happened because you did not seek Me first." Those words rang in my mind over and over for days to come. To this day, I still hear them every time I am faced with the question of what I am to do. His guidance in that one phrase has allowed me to seek a path that I have never imagined for myself. It has allowed me to keep on His Path for my whole life. It has taken me a lifetime to get here, but I now have the tools to overcome anything the enemy could throw at me. Self Doubt, fear, disobedience, self-control problems, and learning to surrender.

I have written three books that I believe God has poured into me, but when I was writing the fourth book, <u>Out of the Ashes: The Flame.</u> He stopped me from writing that book to write this one. I contemplated going on and finishing <u>The Flame</u> and then diving into this one, but the message is too heavy. I needed to speak it to others now. I have learned the hard way that when God speaks and tells you directly to do or not do something, you better listen because if you don't act now, He will remove His Favor from you to find someone who will be obedient. By not doing as God had instructed, I was removing myself from His Will. After everything I had been through, not being in His Will any longer would hurt worse. I never want to be out of His Will again.

After God showed me that I was His Beloved and that He sent His son to die for me so that I may live a life more abundantly, He birthed in me the stories about the dragons. Now, before you start hyperventilating and spewing at me that dragons are evil, God created all creatures. At the beginning of time, He made them, and with Adam, they named them. He said they were good, and He smiled. He made us all, and we all are given to our mother's womb pure and innocent. We are then born into a life of sin and flesh. We, like the dragons in <u>Out of the Ashes,</u> have lived a life before sin, then the darkness hurt us and changed our course. It then became our choice whether we are to walk a life of righteousness and in the Light with God or to follow the fallen dragon of evil and exile ourselves to hell.

God is all-knowing, always present, and will always want you to be by His Side, but He won't force you. He loves you too much to make you do anything. His favor and blessings will not be with you if you choose to sin, but He is always listening for your voice when you're ready to come home and listen to Him. So, when God began to speak to me about my health, I knew that I had to listen and be obedient. He had already proven that He was true and that He wanted what was best for me. It was then that I had to learn to surrender everything to God. Ever since my divorce, my right eye had a cataract in it that made my vision blurry. It was very frustrating. So my heart was in trouble and now my eyes. I wanted to get fixed what I could. My quality of life was degrading as time went on and I had to do something to make it better. So I had my right cataract fixed. Easy in and out outpatient surgery. But right after that surgery was done my left eye detached.

The doctors told me that to repair my eyes then, I would need to go into surgery and be put under anesthesia. They weren't sure that my heart would be able to handle the stress of anesthesia and going under the knife. The enemy started to torment me. It took the doctors and hospitals seven months to approve the surgery, not to mention the stress tests and other things they had to do to give them the most data to predict what my heart might do in a simple reattachment eye surgery.

Seven months went by, and the attacks on my mind and

body continued. With all that God had already shown me and taught me, I was still susceptible to the lies of the enemy. My sleep was messed with. My heart and vascular systems began to panic. I began to retain water. Mobility became almost impossible. My husband had to transport me in a wheelchair. I was not doing good. Mentally. Physically. I was done. I could not take anymore.

It was then that God used a young man in church. He came to the front and said that he had a word from God for someone who was exhausted and needed healing to come forward and receive prayer. I, being one of our church's leaders, wasn't going to admit that I had been struggling with the lies of the enemy. I wasn't going to share with my church family that I felt like dying and that my loved ones were better off without me and my infirmities. I wasn't going to share with them that I couldn't even go to the bathroom any longer without help from my husband. I was in a very bad place, and the worst thing was that the enemy had me believing that it would look bad on God if I told anyone the truth about the thoughts going on in my head. That everyone would think that God had abandoned me. All I kept hearing was the hate Job's friends said to him about his struggles, and I refused to allow the enemy to get any glory from my present situation. So I suffered in silence. Alone. Desperate. I suffered.

It wasn't till he got no answers to his call for this person to come to the front that he came forth again, pleading for that person to come forth to get prayer, and he said that this person thought to themselves that their sleep was their reset button and that they justified that if I could just get good sleep, then everything would be okay. Those words tore through me as a hot rock shot into butter. I knew I had to go up. I mustered all the strength in my legs and body to walk four rows to stand in front of this young man while he was still pleading with the person to come forth. Our pastor told the young man to give me the microphone because I also had a word. But what the pastor didn't realize was that I was there to answer the call, not give one. The young man gave me the microphone, and all I could say was something to the effect that if God was pleading for them to come receive prayer and that I could come up, then so should they. I gave a small testimony to what I was going through and the fear that was killing me regarding the surgery, and then they came around me to pray. That was on the Sunday before the surgery that was to take place on the following Tuesday.

I went into the surgery, having told my loved ones all I needed to say because I truly believed that I was not going to see them again. I knew going into it that I was going to die, and I surrendered everything to God because I was done. There was nothing more I could do to save myself. I went into the surgery with the mindset that if it were God's Will, let it be. What happened was nothing short of a miracle. As soon as I woke from the anesthesia medicines, I knew something was different. Of course, I was encouraged to move slowly and take it easy. The next thing I heard was that my blood sugars had gone low during the procedure, and they were having a hard time getting them to stabilize. Now I know they are doctors and trained nurses, so for them to ask me how to get them to come up was to wake me and get me to respond to their questions. So I said for them to get me a protein shake. In my life, these have been the best way to stabilize my blood sugar quickly and not have the horrible skyrocketing issues later.

As the evening progressed, I kept telling Paul something was different in my heart. I could breathe and not feel labored. I could feel my blood moving better in my veins. My head no longer hurt. Now, granted, my eye hurt like crazy. I just had surgery on it, but other than that, I was feeling better than I had felt in years. I was even able to walk across the room and down the hallway to go to the bathroom without stopping every five minutes to restore the energy that I had just exerted.

However, when my blood sugars were going up, I had to fight them to release me. They have their lies; we'll leave that argument for another time but for the most part. Let's just say they didn't want me to go home. But wouldn't tell me why. First, it was my blood sugar. Then they said it was because my oxygen levels wouldn't stay up. They said it wasn't safe to go home at this time. But when I got to my room, they never hooked me to a monitor to follow my heart or my oxygen levels. The only time I saw someone was when they wanted me to take medicines that I refused to take. I didn't have high cholesterol levels ever in my life. There was no reason for me to take medicine for a problem I didn't have. They wanted to give me blood clot shots to keep my body from creating a blood clot, but I was already on two blood thinners that were making it hard to breathe. They never had a sound answer to any of my questions, and I refuse to do something just because another person tells me it's what is best for me. That morning, I told them they had till noon to run their tests, but after that, I was walking out of there against their wishes. There was no reason to keep me there when this procedure was supposed to be an outpatient one. For all you doctors and nurses out there, yes. I am a difficult patient. I have had to deal with people running over me my whole life. I have had my fair share of abusive and unnecessary medical charges, and I know my rights. Please spare me the eye roll…

The doctor who came on the floor that morning for the ICU did not care. She came in and said she did not need to hear it; she was releasing me as soon as they could get the paperwork processed. Now, I know that seems harsh, but when you have a patient like me in your care, you better be on your A-game. You better be prepared to know the answers to questions or at least be humble enough to say that you don't know the answer, but you will ask someone else who might. She was short in her greeting to me, but she knew I was already upset. At the last minute, my heart doctor sent me a message asking me to stay just to get an ECHO of my heart before I left. He wanted to be sure that everything was okay with my heart before I went home.

I agreed and went to my follow-up eye doctor's appointment before driving back over the mountain to see my family. You have to remember, I went into the surgery knowing I was never going to see my daughter again. My mother, my brothers, my stepson. My nieces, nephews, and cousin...I could go on. I desperately wanted to get home and hug my baby girl's neck. I went into the hospital thinking I was not coming out of there and if I did it would be as my spirit went to be with the Lord. I settled with the fact that I was not going to live any longer. So I was in a hurry.

I want to go back to the torment I was allowing myself to go through before going into the surgery. The enemy had me convinced that I was going to die if I listened to God. He even tried to tell me I was listening to the wrong voice, that he was God and the other voice was satan. But even as the enemy was lying to me and his voice was tormenting me to believe his lies, I knew I had to follow God's Voice. I had to follow the voice that gave me peace. I had to follow the voice that gave me hope. Even though I could not understand how it would be possible for me to live a better life on the other side of the surgery, I knew that I had to go through with it. The one voice was telling me that the surgery would fix my eye and that everything would be okay. That God was going to bring me through it. The other voice was telling me that the surgery was going to kill me. That my heart could not handle the stress of the procedure. I felt hope and peace with one voice, but it never said anything more. Where the other voice wouldn't shut up. It would say things like, "I'm trying to save you; like I did when I told you not to get the bypass surgery." And "Okay don't listen to me, this will be over soon and you can come home." I couldn't tell which one was the right one anymore. I was exhausted weighing the options and truths out in my mind. I settled with the facts. I love the Lord and I need to have my retina reattached so that I can see. If God says that it is my time to go, then He will walk me through whatever may come. It was just to reattach my left retina so that I could see out of that eye again, right?

The enemy had me terrified that I was going to die from this simple procedure. He had me believing that my heart couldn't handle the stress the surgery was going to place on my heart. He had disrupted my sleep with his tormenting lies and worries. Every night I was on my knees before God begging Him to take the anxieties from me so that I could get the rest that I needed. It was a rough time for me. My heart was only putting out maybe 25% of the blood needed for the rest of my body. So my ability to function well was diminished greatly. I always felt like I needed more rest, sleep, and time to recover than a person should at my age. Sleep was valuable to me and my ability to function well the next day. A harsh reality settled in…I may only be forty-four years old, but my body was on its deathbed.

Over time, I had lost all hope that I had that I was one day going to be able to do the things I wanted to do with my life. I had millions of things I wanted to do. Places to go. Foods to eat. Cultures to experience. There were so many things I wanted to see with my own eyes. I didn't want to see the world through the internet or National Geographic Magazine any longer. I had aspirations of a person I thought God turning me into. I had visions of myself speaking to large groups of women and helping them discover the strength to become who they were supposed to be. At first, I was afraid of the vision God showed me, but after a while, I started to see myself through His Heart and I liked what I saw. I saw these things and had no clue before the surgery how I would ever be enough to be who God called me to be.

That's when I realized that I was looking through the wrong lens. Even now after all that God had taught me, He was still fixing my perspective on life. In my first book, My Beloved, He showed me that I was worthy of love, peace, and prosperity in His Eyes. The lessons through that horrible time in my life were unforgettable. But if I must be honest. That was only the beginning of the tearing down of the hard shell I had made around my heart. He was still working on me and I still had a long road ahead of me.

I walked into that operating room pre-op area barely breathing. I was too afraid of what was coming next. Was it going to hurt? I settled with the idea that they were going to put me to sleep and I just was never going to wake up. I would fade away and step into a life with God by my side. No more sorrow. No more pain, right? Little did I know that the surgery was over and now the real work was about to begin. I had scheduled an appointment with my heart doctor because even a week after my ECHO I still could not get the result of the tests. I wanted to know what it said was wrong with my heart.

You see I was used to something always being wrong that I couldn't grasp the fact that something good had happened during that surgery. So when the doctor came in to tell me his news it still took a while for it to sink in. He told me he didn't have an explanation but it appears that my heart was healed! It was now pumping blood at a normal heart's range! I knew something felt weird but completely healed?!? Was he serious? I told him how I had been feeling. How I could walk further than I had been able to in years. How the medicines made my stomach and head hurt. If I was healed, then couldn't I stop taking them? After all, why treat a condition that was no longer there, right? He said that his training says that I should still keep taking my medicines but he would respect my choices as I moved forward. He would still care for my treatments when the time arose.

I was stunned silent. God healed my heart! But yet I still felt like I shouldn't accept the news yet. That there was a shoe that was getting ready to drop. I just knew there was something bad that was going to take this away from me. My husband was a different story. He wanted to shout it to the whole neighborhood. As we left the hospital and out to lunch, he said to me, "Now you know what you have to do, right?" I knew what he was referring to. I had to testify. I should want to testify, right? I should want to tell the world that my God, My King did the impossible for me. Surgeons all said there was nothing they could do to help my heart aside from a full heart transplant and even then they didn't know if I would recover from it. They were settled in the action to take all these medicines and pray for the best until I went to be with the Lord. My doctor, the same man, who had six months ago told my husband that he should lay off encouraging me to be more active because there was nothing they could do to heal my heart and that he should spend as much time as he could with me while he still had time, was now saying he doesn't know how it happened but its healed. Just like that, done. BAM!

God didn't just help me through a rough time of my life, HE HEALED IT! When man was out of options, BAM! God Worked His Handiwork! When man gave up hope...BAM! God was able to work! I had to go to Him and ask Him if this was real. Somehow, I thought that I needed clarification on His Truth for my life. What He said was profound to me. He said,

"Now the real work begins."

And in that moment I knew my journey was beginning. After years of standing still. Through a horrible divorce and custody battle. After watching many prophets, speakers, and ministers come through my church being used to share the gospel. Hearing saints and sinners give testimonies of the work God was doing in their lives. Seeing great ministers and friends fall from their podium into controversy, backsliding, and sin. I was instructed by God to stand still and wait. I wanted to speak out, but God said no. I wanted to preach, but God said no. I wanted to teach, but God said no. I wanted to help, but God said no. I wanted to step into the greatness God was showing me and yet He kept saying no, don't move. I came to the conclusion years ago that I was someone who was meant to make God great from behind the scenes and that was where I settled.

After twenty years, He now was saying testify to the church about what I have done here. I couldn't move. I couldn't think. All I knew was that I had told my pastor I needed to testify next Sunday and he said okay. He asked me how long it would take. I knew my husband had already shared with him the news because he couldn't wait any longer to tell someone... How could I prepare a message on His Work in me? I had so many things rolling around in my head about what it was I could say. Connections I could make in scripture to use in my sermon. Metaphors galore about how God worked. That Sunday I had a plan of attack to bring my testimony to life. I was going to correlate it in three different ways. First, I was going to speak on what men said was possible. Then talk about the strength of David to not do what man said and listen to God instead. Second, I was going to talk about my fears and what the enemy was doing in my head. Third, I was going to end up with the healing. But as the service moved forward one person from the praise and worship team gave the word I had about David and listening to God. So I had to scratch that off my sermon. Then someone talked about the lies of the enemy and fears he would use...Another point scratched off my list. All I was left with was me sharing my example of being obedient and surrendering to the Lord all I was struggling with before my surgery. All I had left was my unprotected heart and God's Glory for what HE had done for me. I gave my testimony. I cried. Shoot, who do I think I am kidding, everyone in the service was balling. We all were a mess, but God wanted them to be invested in my story. So there I was laid bare for all to see. Vulnerable. Cut open and human. But when we can learn to let go and give God the chance to be glorified that's when we truly can say it's all about Him.

The weeks after that testimony are a whirlwind. I say that because God started to pour into me more and more each day. The closer to Him I got the more He spoke about what He wanted me to say and where we were going. That's when this book started to unfold before my eyes. I had a vision of the book's cover design and when I saw it a spark was ignited deep into my soul. I had a vision early on after my surgery about the moments before his fight with Goliath where David leaned down to pick up his five stones.

The vision was in slow motion. Every stone he picked up, I felt in my heart the mantle and weight of what lesson each stone carried on his soul and mind. As David sighed to pick the stone up, he walked through the painful lessons he had overcome to be where he now was. Each stone represented a heavy lesson God had taught him about who he was and the mantle that he carried for God. The rocks were light but the lessons were heavy. As he picked up the next stone a new lesson struck his heart and got heavier to carry but his spirit was fortified with power and strength. His experiences and triumphs were with him as he walked to stand before Goliath. An uncircumcised Philistine threatening God's People on the battlefield in front of him. With each stone, David marked a memorial of his life and lessons to God and the journey of what God had brought him through.

So as he stood there before Goliath with no armor, shield, or sword he was not afraid for God had already prepared him for this fight. Those five stones that David picked up were the weapons that he used to tear down his enemies. Those five stones he held in his hands were the tools God gave him to walk into God's Greatness. Those five stones were his stepping stones to step into God's Favor. Every person's walk with God is different but there is always the same battle in our soul. We have to learn to overcome the world and remove sin from our lives so that we can be more like Christ. We have to learn to be obedient in our walk with Him. We have to learn to listen to His Ways above all others to set our feet on solid ground. Then and only then can we find out who we are in Him. Then we can walk into Biblical greatness.

Easier said than done, right? I have been a Christian all of my life and if I am being honest with you now, I still felt unworthy of holding a microphone and leading others to walk with God. Who was I to tell others about God? Why would anyone want to hear what I have to say about the King of Kings and Lord of Lords? On that stage while I gave my testimony and that question came to my mind in the middle of an awkward moment to pause, He gave me the answer. It's not about you or what you could do or say. It's all about Me...The I AM.

In that moment, all the self-doubt, worry, and fear went away. I did nothing to help myself. I tried to lose the weight because the doctors said it would heal me. Nothing worked. I took the medicines they said to take to heal me. Nothing worked. I rested because they said to rest. I drank water because they said I was dehydrated. I stopped drinking because I was swelling. I was not as active then I was. I did everything I was told to do. I did everything I knew to do. Nothing I did healed my heart.

You see, my healing was not because I did something. I was healed because God healed me and in all my lessons did nothing for me until I learned that crucial point in my walk with God. There was nothing I could say or do but testify to the truth. There was no magical potion or concoction that could heal me. There was no recipe for greatness. There was nothing I could buy, smoke, grow, drink, or inhale that could bring my heart back to life. Only GOD could heal me. He was God and I was not. I didn't have to pretend that I had it all together because I knew that I didn't. God wanted them to see that.

He brought me back to my vision of David and his stones.

The first stone was David's self-doubt. How could God be glorified in David's life if he walked around like I was walking and talking? What if David walked around ashamed of his weight and height? What if he spoke negative affirmations over himself the way that I was? What if he compared himself to his eight older brothers and sold himself short that he wasn't going to amount to anything because of the troubles that life had dealt him?

At this time I was writing the book <u>The Flame</u> and I was researching how a blacksmith creates a shield out of a sheet of metal. One of my dragons was a slave under an owner who was a blacksmith and God was speaking and using him in a mighty way to create armor for a warrior later in the book. His lessons spoke to me through the Word in such a magnificent way. I was writing about the Refiner's Fire and how a blacksmith knows when the heating of the metal, gold, or silver is done on the fire and removing the impurities in the metal...Do you know how long to hold metal over a fire and know when it is finished? A blacksmith melts the iron, gold, or silver down and it is done in the flame when the blacksmith can see his reflection on the surface. Come on!!! It still blows up in my spirit and mind when I think about it. God holds us in the flame until all the impurities are gone and He can see HIS FACE reflected in us! God's Lessons and Fires purify our walk and make us righteous so that we can reflect HIS GLORY to HIM!

God doesn't look at us and want to see the bad that we do! He doesn't want to see our possessions, our money, or our houses or cars. He wants to look at us and see His Righteousness, His Glory, His Perfection! We are held in the flame until we are done. So I had to question myself...Does God see Himself in the way I walk or talk? Does He look down and see glory, honor, and holiness? Am I worthy in His Eyes to receive His Praise? Or am I reflecting to Him only the lies the enemy is speaking in my ears? The filth, the shame, the hurt, the unworthiness, the damnation the world has attached to me. Furthermore, what is my heart reflecting to the world if I am reflecting those things to God?

How could I ever expect God to use me in a great way if I perceived myself so shamefully? I couldn't. So it was then and there I went on a slow overhaul of the image that I carried of myself. I had to learn to carry the confidence the same way an ambassador for a king would carry themselves. I had to learn to carry myself with dignity and honor that was worthy of my King. In that process, I also learned to refine my speech. I had to slow down my speech. I talked too much, too fast.

Anyone who knows me, I speak from the hip and when I start talking I don't always know when to stop. I am like the song that never ends. I go on and on, my friend. Sorry, I am just joking but honestly, it's the truth. When I am trying to make a point, it always takes me a long time to get there because there are always so many things that flood into my mind when I am talking. I want you to know every detail that brought me to where I am. So I have had to learn to put my thoughts through the fire and only speak what makes it through the fire. With every success I experienced, I got more confident in who I was in God.

Remember my heart was healed but my body was still struggling and God told me to include everyone in my journey. So I began sharing on Facebook. One of the first things He said was to Exercise my Faith. The title correlated as a metaphor to me in two different ways. My doctor said my body was like one of a coma patient who had just woke up from laying in a bed in a coma for three years. The muscles were depleted of their strength and had not been used for so long. So I had to get active and get moving again. Which spoke to me in the spirit as well as my physical needs.

As Christians, our pastors speak to us every Sunday about the perceptions of a so-called Christian life but what if we heard them the wrong way? We heard go forth and make fishers of men; so we taught them how to fish and how to lead little children to God within the four walls of our Church, or to speak at a men's conference, or a leadership seminar, but what if God meant to go out into the community to reach those who don't know God and teach them about the ways of God? What if we heard that we are to lay down for our brothers and sisters in Christ, so we began to listen and forgive them because God forgave us. But what if God meant to literally lay down for them and give them our backs as a stepping stone away from their troubles? What if our hearing the Word is not what God meant when He said He wanted to change the world? What if HE wanted us to go out and change the way the World thought about us? Change how they feel about themselves? Change the way the world sees Him? If we are a pure and perfect reflection of God, our Father in Heaven, then our friendships here on Earth should also reflect Him and our relationship with Him. If a blacksmith knows that the silver is pure and no longer full of impurities because he can see his reflection on the surface, then shouldn't the world be seen through God's Eyes in the same way? What if we are supposed to be more? To do more for others? What if we aren't meant to stay in our little lanes but what if we were called to share our revelations with others? Tell those people at the gas station what God is doing in your life right now. What if you're supposed to go to a community picnic and share who God is with someone who needs to know Him?

Shouldn't our relationship with each other be holy and

reflect God's Glory to its fullest? Yes, that is the answer that I am looking for. God calls us to bring others who are not believers to Him and convince them through our love and grace that HE is God and that He is the only way, the only truth, and the only light worth following. I know it's easier said than done, right? How can we pull aside the unrepentant sinner and say your way is the wrong way? Even though the world says that it's okay for them to live that way. As long as they aren't hurting others then we don't need to worry about their sins, their decisions, or their mistakes in their thoughts. The law of man says they have the right to believe in whatever makes them feel good about who they are. If they want to kill themselves working eighty hours a week for that money, then let them. If they want to pray to the god of grass because they know it's real and answers their prayers, then let them, right? They aren't hurting anyone else, so why is how and what they believe any of your business? If they want to love and have sex with another man, then let them, right? If they want to love and have sexual relations with another female, then let them, right? You don't have to be in the same bed as them, so let them, right?

I know. These questions are hard. They were hard for me to answer for my own understanding of what God thought about these things. Even when I went to the scriptures I found no glorious light or consolation prize to all my questions. Other than God called these things sin and wrong in His Eyes. Everything that I found that spoke on the matter said for me to depart from them and to wipe my feet clean of them. But that was not the heart of God; not of the God I knew. At least not the Heart and Soul of the Living God I knew and loved. How could I sit back and know with every fiber of my being that my God loved me and called me His

Beloved and then turn my back on others I knew He also loved and died on the cross for? How could I leave them in this filthy pit of depressive hate and turmoil? I felt like a hypocrite. Furthermore, I had loved ones living and believing these lies to their core. How could I leave them in this suffering? What did that say about me? What does that say about my God and King? That's when I came across the scripture that tells us to pull our brothers and sisters to the side in private and show them in love how they are wrong in their sins. God tells us to show them a loving way back to the fold.

God has told me my whole life that I never had to defend my faith because God's Word was true and just. He always told my heart that He didn't need me to argue His Truths to the unbeliever. He said that I just had to show them His Love, Grace, and Mercy. I had to show them that He was real by what He did for me and tell them about it. It wasn't until He told me to write my books that I was told to say more. At the beginning of this journey, God told me to be ready to speak about His Truths. Long story short, I had to know God's Heart and be able to tell others about what He meant.

This leads me back to my vision of David. The first stone that David had to overcome was his self-doubt. God began to show me the obstacles that David had in his heart about being a strong warrior for God. The Scriptures don't tell us specifically about his time before he came into Saul's court except to tell us that Samuel was led to Jesse's house to find the new king. However, there were many prophecies in scripture about the coming of Our Savior and in those prophecies, God reveals His Truths about David to us. All I will say about the matter now is that God showed me the truth of it all and you will find that his life was not that much different than ours. He fought with others about his faith, and his place to belong in his community, and he wanted love just like they did. He had father issues and he loved his mother even though his father no longer loved them.

Jesse, David's father, had eight strong boys before God gave him David. The three older brothers were strong warriors in Saul's Army. The scriptures tell us that before that moment one of God's Prophets, Samuel, had come to Jesse's house because God said to him that Saul's replacement king would come from one of Jesse's sons. So Samuel obediently went there to look for him. To anoint the one God led him to.

Samuel asked Jesse to bring his sons before him and as they stood there, Samuel dismissed them from his presence. He then asks Jesse if there were any other sons and Jesse says yes, there was one more but he was out in the field tending to the sheep. Samuel asks that he be brought right away and David comes. Samuel sees God's Glory resting on David and he knows how to move forward.

That's what scripture tells us when we read specifically about David and his path to kingship in 1st and 2nd Samuel. What we tend to forget is that there were many different players in any one given story. We see ourselves in singular form. Me, myself, and I got us to where we are. Sure, some people walked with us for a short time but they were not the ones walking my destiny out. Sure, some players affected our game and changed some of the details but I decided to take the path that got me where I am.

Or in some minds, they blame everyone else for the bad decisions that brought them to the pile of ashes that they lie in. Regardless it is never the truth of the matter. We would have to live a life completely cut off from everyone in the world to say we did it all on our own. So can be said of

David's life. You have to remember that David, son of Jesse was listed in the lineage of Jesus Christ, son of God. David was only a small part of a very big picture. The story of good versus evil.

So we can trust that God had more to tell us about David's life. More than we read just in Samuel's part of David's succession into becoming King of Israel. To understand the mindset of young David, to know where he was and how he overcame these struggles we need to go back more than eleven generations before his birth.

We need to go all the way back to Moses' time to understand what David was going through. We have to understand the culture of their time so that we can have some revelation of his troubles that he was living through. So we know that God's People upset God and were sent into a forty-year stint of walking through the wilderness in the Desert of Paran before they could be delivered into the Promised Land in Jerusalem that God told them He would deliver them to. At the end of that forty-year hike, God meets with Moses on Mount Sinai to be given the Ten Commandments and other laws to govern God's People.

These Commandments, these six hundred and thirteen commandments were guiding laws for God's People to be set apart from other tribes and countries across the world. The story is listed in Exodus, but the laws are spread through Genesis, Exodus, Leviticus, Numbers, and Deuteronomy. However, the ruling that we are to reflect on for this part of David's history is the one listed in Deut. 23:2. It states that.

"No one born of a forbidden marriage, nor any of their descendants may enter the assembly of the Lord, not even the tenth generation."

* * *

Now, this curse is brought on any house if a man or woman has sexual relations with anyone outside of the marital union. This commandment was given to God's People in 1406 BC, but the law was not broken by Jesse's forefathers until 1446 in Judah and Tamar.

Judah had a son, his firstborn, and his name was Er. Er was married to a Canaanite woman by the name of Tamar. However, before they could have any children, God found Er to be wicked and had him killed. In God's Law, if they did not have children to secure her place and name in Judah's home, Er's brother Onan was to marry her and give her children after Er died. Onan did not want that and after having sexual relations with her several times, he withdrew and made his seed fall to the ground. Refusing to give her children and disobeyed God. So God had him killed as well. Judah only had one son left with Shua and he was too young to fulfill his role for his father. So Judah told Tamar to return to her father's house and wait for him to come of age. So she did as she was told.

Many years later, Judah went to a nearby city to have his sheep's wool sheered. The person who cut the wool heard that Judah was visiting and went to tell Tamar of his arrival. However, when Judah got there she realized that Judah's son, Shua, was already of age and she still had not yet been called to return. Upset that her place and security were taken from her, she got dressed as a Shrine prostitute and veiled her face to stand nearby where Judah was getting his sheep's wool cut. She is called by Judah to come and sleep with him and she agrees if he pays her. He promises to give her a goat for her services. She agrees only if he gives her his seal, cords, and staff as a pledge till she is paid. He does so and he goes on his way.

Judah sent his friend back into the town with the goat to

pay the prostitute but, she was nowhere to be found. Unaware she was his daughter-in-law, he shrugs the ordeal off his mind. Until the town realizes that Tamar is pregnant and not married. Accused of being promiscuous and ordered to be burned to death according to Jewish law, she hands the elders the seal, cords, and staff of the man who was the father to hold him accountable. Judah recognizes the items and counts her more righteous than he and orders her to be released. She secures her right to Er's belongings and her place in history. Because her son Perez led to David. However, the deception used by Tamar and the unholy sexual relations of this union activated the Bastard Curse upon Jesse's Family Line as described in Deut. 23:2.

From that unholy union, she brought forth ten generations of shame upon the bloodline of Jesse. Her family bloodline continued through her son, Perez, and on into the family line of Jesse. That shame brought on her family meant they could not gather with other Israelites during times of fellowship or times when their communities would gather for ceremonies before the Lord. So after their union, their family carried the shame and guilt of that union upon their lives. They would have been shunned; people would turn their backs on them when they walked by. They would refuse to talk to them or help them if they were in need.

Now in today's day and age, it is easy to be ignored. People walk through the mall and do not say hello to anyone while shopping. But you have to remember that back in that time everything was done at the town market. You did your food shopping from vendors there. You bought all your needs from another person who made, sold, or created those goods to sell to you. You needed to communicate with the people to buy your supplies to live. So those descendants probably felt like our homeless people do today. Ashamed at how they looked. Condemned by that shame. Exiled to live outside the town limits; away from everyone else. Which would have led to them feeling unsafe and vulnerable to attacks. They would have felt like an outcast.

So growing up as an outcast from the Israeli community, David probably spent a lot of time alone without friends around him. His point of view about the world and how it worked probably looked vastly different from others around him. Even his older brothers more than likely treated him differently.

Now I have tried to find out the truth of the curse and how it played out exactly in David's life but I can't find the answers in scripture. Was the bastard curse a curse that meant that there would not be any faithful men in that family line? Or was the one unholy union of Judah and Tamar the only indiscretion and the pains were felt by everyone who followed? I couldn't find the answer, but I looked into the lines and just like any other family line, there were good men and bad men. There were good wives and bad wives that led up to David's birth. However, I did find a writing that was uncovered and reported by the Museum of Jewish People (Cit. 1) that did clarify some of the confusion and it correlated with everything I have found and seen so far about his history.

Jesse, David's father, had only married one woman in his life. Her name was Nitzevet. She was a faithful Hebrew woman raised in the traditions and culture. She was not unfaithful and did not have an affair on Jesse. However, after so many years of being married to her, Jesse had pulled himself from her for three years. It was reported that he had fallen in love with Nitzevet's maid. One day when his temptation grew to be too much for him, he went to her and told her about his feelings. He says that he wants her and asks her to lay with him and to prepare herself to come to his bed. Appalled and faithful to her mistress, Nitzevet, she runs to her and tells her what Jesse had divulged to her in secret. However, she does not get upset instead, she tells her maid to do as he asks but as she removes the light from the room they switch places at the last second. Jesse thinks he has relations with the maid but instead, he is having relations with his wife. Unaware of the betrayal, they go on with life. But in several months when his wife starts to show he realizes he had been fooled. The writer doesn't tell us any emotions or reactions that were recorded but the scriptures tell us everything that we need to know about their relationship as David grew up.

When God sent Samuel to Jesse's house to find the new king to replace Saul, Samuel asked Jesse to come and sacrifice to the Lord and to bring his sons. So Jesse gathers his sons and they go to meet with Samuel to make the sacrifice. When Samuel sees the eldest son, Eliab, he appears to be the obvious choice to be king according to his stature. However, God says that he has rejected him and for Samuel to not worry about their outward appearance. Man looks at someone's looks but God looks at their heart.

Once Samuel has been told that none of these men are the ones chosen by God to be king, Samuel questions Jesse once more. Are there no more sons in your house? Jesse answers, "Yes, there is one more in the field tending the sheep." I have read several translations and the words aren't there, but I have always felt like Jesse never thought that much of David. I have always felt like Jesse forgot to call David. That he was ashamed of him. Or maybe he just wasn't worthy or strong enough in Jesse's eyes? How could you forget that you have a son? How could Jesse not call David in from the field when he called the others?

If you think about the circumstances of his birth—the fact that his mother was no longer loved by Jesse and that his eyes were for another. The mere fact that he was tricked into having sex with her could not have made it easy on David. Jesse was a man with passion for another woman and his wife took her from him. His wife made him stay righteous when in fact Jesse wanted to sin with the maid. Any man would have been outraged. He spent three years pushing Nitzevet away from himself. He no longer loved her. He no longer wanted her body or pleasure.

I don't know if you have ever been pushed away from someone who should have loved you but it's very painful. You want their love, attention, their touch. Everything you do, you do it praying that they will come back to you. That they will see you and love you again. However, the one who has pushed you away has built nothing for you except hatred in his heart. He has to turn away from you, because you remind him of his disgraceful actions and no amount of justification can ever make it right again. No matter how many lies he tells himself, what he did to you to betray you was evil and until he makes that right with you and with God he will always feel bad about what he did. So when he looked at David, he saw the mud on his face. I would imagine that Jesse sent David out in the fields to tend to the sheep because he couldn't stand seeing the reminder of the sin on his heart. Like I said before, everything we do is reflected to the Lord. So what was Jesse reflecting to God? Was his heart pure and holy? Or had evil crept its way into Jesse's life in a small moment of weakness? God tells us in Proverbs 27:19,

"As is water face reflects face, So a man's heart reveals the man."

Proverbs 21:2 says,

* * *

"Every way of a man is right in his own eyes, but the Lord weighs the heart."

The only conclusion I can come to with full assurance regarding the bastard's curse that was on Jesse's bloodline is that when David came of age and stood before Samuel, God's Favor was on him. I can't tell you how the curse manifested through the men before David. Did the curse mean that the family was physically separated and not allowed to fellowship with other believers for ten generations? Or did that mean that God removed His Presence from their lives? As to say that they could no longer hear the voice of God. We don't have detailed accounts of all the men who lived in Jesse's family before David, but we do know that in David's life, he heard the voice of God speak to him. Only three men in Adam's family bloodline were described as being able to hear from God directly. There was Adam. There was Noah. Then there was Abraham. Abraham had two generations after him before Judah and Tamar's troubles where the bastard's curse was laid on their family line. Ten generations passed before David and none of them are described as having the ability to hear from God.

It tells us in 1 Samuel and 2 Samuel that David asked God and God answered him. We don't have the historical accounts of the ten generations before him written in the scriptures but we do have his life to pull from. So scripture tells us that David heard the Lord, just like we can hear Him today if we call on His Name. We read how God's Favor was over him as a young man with the lion, the bear, and then with Goliath. We read how David was full of integrity, a man after God's Heart. He could hear the guidance of God in his heart and his mind. I can't say that the prior generations could but given the fact none of them came into God's Greatness and Glory the way David did, we can safely say, that hearing God speak was vital to David's success.

God's Voice molded David to know who he was through God's Eyes. I believe that God separated David from the community and away from his brothers so that he wouldn't be distracted by the things of the world but would learn to hear God's Voice. Because David could hear God's Voice and was guided by Him to do great things. God trained him to trust His Voice to overcome the lion. God trained David to follow His Voice to overcome the bear. God spoke to David in his quiet time to teach him the ways of the Lord. Not just talking to God but listening to His Answers. The only way we can understand who God is and to learn how we can please Him, is to listen to Him.

We have to stop and understand His Heart. We have to learn what He expects from us. We have to understand why He asks us to act, think, and speak His Way. The more we can understand who He is the closer we will be to glorifying Him the best we can here on Earth. We will never be able to reflect to Him a righteous and holy image if we don't become more like Him. So we have to remain in God's Refining Fire until all of our impurities are gone. We have to let go of the sin that tempts us, push away the distractions that keep us from walking out the path that He intended for us, and we have to learn that trusting Him is the only way we can achieve greatness. He is the way, the truth, and the light. We are the best version of ourselves with Him guiding us. We have to learn to be obedient to His Call.

Chapter Two: Obedience

2

As a mom, there are many requests in my house. However, there are a few rules I demand that must be obeyed. I only have one phrase I repeat to every child that enters my home. "I should only have to ask you once to do something." In my eyes, respect goes both ways. If you want me to respect your wishes, then you need to respect mine. If I work hard to give you a safe place to live. I provide food, shelter, clothing, toys, entertainment, drinks, schooling, phones, computers, books, etc, for you, then the least you can do for me is respond the first time I ask you to do something.

For my natural-born children, this wasn't a hard rule because they grew up with the expectations that I had of them. However, that cannot be said for the children who came to my home unwillingly. I say unwillingly because we have taken in foster children, and their circumstances were not of their choosing. They did not choose for me to love them. They did not choose for me to guide them. They did not want my help, and any offering of peace always came with a hard-fought "Hell no!" followed by a loud slam of a door and an exclamation mark!

I see people who have not accepted God as their Lord and Savior as the foster care children of Heaven. They do not understand the love that comes from instruction. They do not want to listen to your house rules because they do not understand why they have them. They cannot comprehend the reasoning for the rule. They see rules as a noose around their necks, keeping them from freedom, joy, and happiness. They do not understand that God is like their caregiver. He wants what's best for them and He wants them to be healthy, safe, and out of trouble. Let us not mention the troubles that lie out there that come from satan himself to keep us from being in God's Will.

This leads me to David's second stone that he leaned down to pick up from the dust. David had to learn to be obedient to God. I will admit this lesson was not a hard one for me to understand because, by the time I had been given the stone for this lesson, God had already taught my heart so much through my children and foster children. Trust me...God helped me understand how to help them through their hard times. If I didn't have God, Lord knows where we all would be right now. There is nothing harder than living the life of a parent.

God brings these children out of some pretty horrible situations and uses your heart, home, and family to show them true love. Something they have never seen before and believe me when I tell you this...These children have seen and heard it all. Every lie. Every excuse. Every petty story that they made up to justify the pain their parents or caregivers put them through. They felt every bit of it, and they held onto it to protect themselves from ever feeling hurt again. It's the mind's way of teaching you quickly to protect yourself from trauma. If you recognize the pain early, then you won't be caught off guard ever again. Therefore never want to allow themselves to be hurt that badly ever again.

The similarities of the characteristics of an unsaved person and a foster child are scary. They both fight tooth and nail for everything they think they deserve, but they can't wrap their mind around the fact that what God and a healthy, good foster parent want are the same things. God wants them to be safe and free from terror. He wants food in their fridge and clean clothes on their backs. He wants them to go to school to learn everything they can so that when they grow up to be an adult, they can have a good job to buy the things they need and want. Most of all, God wants them to know that they are loved beyond human comprehension. He wants them to be hugged, kissed, worried about, celebrated, and adored. However, just as those parents lied to their children, so has the world and the enemy lied to the unbeliever, and until someone comes along and proves God's Truth to them as safe, they will continue to protect themselves the best way they can.

~ * ~

Proving God's Love is harder than it sounds. Both for the foster parents who are trying to show love to a kid who has been neglected and for the Christian trying to show love to an unbeliever. Without God's Help, it can't be done. On either front. At least not effectively. As I learned the hard way when caring for a young man, we'll call Donovan. The name Donovan means Dark Warrior, and that was the heart of this young man when he first came to us. When he first came to live with us, he presented himself as someone who would be easy to care for. That he was just an innocent boy who hung around with the wrong kind of people. One who knew he was making big mistakes, according to what you believed was his truth. He was a young teen, and as many of you know, at that age, they know everything and that all they have to do is get free of you before they can prove you all wrong. On everything. Donovan was sure he was ready for the world and what it had to offer him.

He was convinced that when he turned eighteen and could move out on his own, he was going to be rolling in money and driving the brand-new Mercedes off the lot. He thought he was the best thing since sliced bread. He was good at being on his own, and we had him all wrong. He said so out of his mouth. He hated us. He all but said so.

I won't go into the details that made him who he is because I feel those details aren't mine to share with the world. But let's just say he learned it all from his situation. The very dynamics of what got him removed from his family to find him a more stable home life. I won't speak to the decisions of his parents because I am not them. They were given every opportunity to correct the problems that led to their son's removal but continued the destructive course despite their children's pleas. Because of the court's decision not to sever the parents' rights from their child, we were ordered to maintain visitation with them. Every other weekend, the chaos, the darkness, and the lies would continue to play out in Donovan's life. So after their visits, we would have to tear down the lies spoken over him, and we would have to repair any new damage that was done. We would have to go in and prove the things they were telling him were not true and that the real truth was what he could see, touch, and feel. We would have to rebuild the foundation of love we had built while showing him that what was being done to him was not healthy and real love. It was an ongoing uphill battle that never showed us any rewards.

It got to be so bad in our home that we had to give him

back to the courts to order constant supervision of him because he had become a constant flight risk. His parents kept saying that they were doing everything the courts had asked of them, but they still wouldn't give him back to them. Which, unfortunately, was just a lie to keep them good to him, but everyone else was the evil keeping them separated. So he would take it upon himself to get back to them. He started running away, and when that started, we had no choice but to concede.

It broke our hearts because, in the end, we felt like we had failed him. We were torn, hurt, damaged, and broken when he left. He was so happy he had gotten his way. He knew that he was going back to the boys' home, but we think that he thought that eventually, he would be going back to his parents. He said some hurtful, ugly things as he left that day. He didn't want anything we had given him. He just wanted his clothes. So my husband went inside to pack his things. However, he did make sure that the Bible we gave him was in the box.

The next few months were painful. The enemy attacked us viciously. The rejection, the loss, and the hurt that stayed with us were unbearable. We used these months to take some time for healing. We loved and ministered to one another, but the pain remained. It wasn't until he went through the hurt that he was never going home to his parents, living with the realization that he was not a priority to his parents, and went to live with his older brother that we saw a change in him and were able to heal ourselves.

When he was with us, everything we taught him was given to him to be able to live life to the fullest without anyone else's help. I taught him that it was better for him to make his meals from fresh ingredients, not full of

41

preservatives and sugars. I taught him that his body needed healthy foods, not food from McDonald's every meal. His body needed the nutrients that a home-cooked meal would give him. Because as a parent, it is our job to raise our children so that we won't have to worry whether or not they will make it. We will know that they can. We want to know that they can do everything we can do, but better. We told him this much. It is not our job to do life for you. When they grow up, we want them to have a clean home, a refrigerator full of food, clean dishes in the cabinets, nice clothes in their closet...We want them to function without help, not that help isn't available to them, but we want them not to need anyone else.

God wants that for all His Children. At the beginning of our relationship with Him, He is there, teaching us the fundamentals of who He is and how He wants things done. He teaches us the rules and why the rules are there. To protect us and to keep us from walking into danger. He teaches us the lies that the enemy is speaking to us. He shows us how satan operates to manipulate and to hurt us. God shows us these things and reveals these hard lessons to us, not to keep us from happiness but to keep us from death and destruction. To keep us from running away from Him and His Will for our lives. His Will for us never changes. He tells us in Jeremiah 29:11,

"For I know the thoughts that I think toward you, says the Lord, thoughts of peace and not of evil, to give you a future and a hope."

God is a Father on His Porch, and we are the child who is running away from Him. We are the Prodigal Son. He told us that we have an inheritance in His House, but all we want to do is spend our money now. We want to live--fast and hard under no supervision or regulations. We want to do it our way because we know how to do it all on our own, without anyone's help. We are reckless, blind to the dangers, and uneducated in the darkness that has roamed this world since the dawn of time. We are just like Donovan... too young to know better and just old enough to get into real trouble with no way out. That's right where satan wants us. In trouble and bound for an eternity in hell with him. Better yet, if he had it his way, we would be six feet under; that way, he wouldn't have to worry about us anymore. End of story. Case closed. So he could move on to the next troubled child of God.

If we can't be obedient to God, our Heavenly Father, here when we are alive, then how could we expect to enter into His Kingdom to be rewarded in Heaven for a job well done? So as we walk with Him, we must listen to His Voice and do as He says to do. If we don't, I feel that God will remove His Favor from us as He did with King Saul. I don't want to go off course with this, but if you would like to read more about King Saul, you can refer to Samuel in the Bible. However, for this chapter, we will not dive deep into all of Saul's life. Only to say that God demands our complete obedience to every part of the Word He Speaks. Not just in spirit, but in truth and all of it. As Saul learned the hard way. Through Samuel, God told King Saul to kill all of the Amalekites. God tells him to kill all that belongs to them. The men, women, children, infants, cattle, and even the donkeys. Maybe Saul didn't think there was any harm in enslaving the king of the Amalekites. Maybe he thought God was His Friend. Who knows? Saul could have just thought God was being a little harsh on the people, that He couldn't have meant to kill them all. We could make every excuse in the book for King Saul, but the scriptures go on to tell us the anger God felt for Saul's disobedience. There was no mistake in what was said. God told Saul to kill everyone. No exceptions. God did not say bring their king back to me and make him your slave. God said to destroy everything. So for Saul's disobedience, God removed His Favor and clarity from Saul's mind. God tells Saul you have been removed as the king of my people. I have chosen another to replace you. Little David enters here... But you see, because Saul could not listen to God, God had no choice but to remove him from His Kingdom.

I don't know about the rest of you, but I had parents that I had to listen to. I would know when I was in trouble. I could feel it enter the room by the look on my mother's face. I could sense it in every extremity. I knew that I had done wrong, and I always knew there were going to be consequences for my actions. Especially the actions that led to my disobeying them. I would have imagined that Saul had the same experience with Samuel and the Lord. Samuel guided Saul and groomed him to become God's King. So when he disobeyed, I could only imagine the disappointment Samuel felt and the look that he gave Saul. I would imagine he felt it in all his extremities as well. Most of when we are in trouble with a parent, we feel shame and remorse. We understand immediately that an apology is due and repentance is to come. We then need to make it right to the best of our ability. We have to do something to show that we are sorry. We need to correct our path, change our ways, or stop doing something that has caused the wrong. But some don't learn things quickly. They allow their pride and arrogance to get in their way. It keeps them from correcting the wrong they've done, and they continue down a path that is not what God wanted for them. Which was where we thought Donovan was when he left our home. We thought he was going to walk a more self-destructive path than he did. So we had to let him go.

Donovan, since then, has come back to talk with us. He has apologized and asked us to forgive him for the things that he had done. He has told us that he was wrong and that we were right. As a child, he acted like a child, but now as a man, he showed us that he had grown up and repented for his wrongdoings. That's what God wants from His Children. He wants them to say, "Father, God, I am sorry for being disobedient and for not listening to you. I know, now that you were just trying to do what was best for me. Forgive me for all my hateful old ways. Please allow me to come home and eat at your table, Lord. We want the meat and food at your table because they make us healthy and strong. We want what you give us, Lord because everything the world has given us has left me feeling sick and starving. Lord, please love me again."

God's rules are not there to keep us from being who we were meant to be. They are there to show us how to grow stronger, be better, to live a fuller and more abundant life without the pain, hurt, and frustration. God tells us that His Yoke is easy and His Burden is light. (Matthew 11:28-30) In my experience, every time I give my struggle over to God, He replaces it with an easier path. Not because I am weak but because He is Strong. Every time I try to overcome a mountain or an obstacle that I feel is more than I can bear, God shows me that there is always an easier way in Him or through His Way.

When I had my heart attacks and I had to close down my store, I was devastated. I was destroyed because I had worked so hard to get there, and I had put in so much time and energy getting my baked goods out there. After three years, I was finally making a profit, and we were headed into a very profitable catering season with weddings right around the corner. I was taking a deep breath one day, and I felt relief because the hard work was finally going to pay off. We were headed into a season of prosperity. I could feel it in my bones. If I were a gambler, I would've bought a lottery ticket because I was sure something great was right around the corner for me.

Little did I know that two nights later would begin the hardest lessons of my spiritual life. My physical life had already experienced the hardest blows life could give me by taking away my husband and my daughter. It wasn't enough because now I had to undergo the hardest spiritual lessons too. I had to learn a deeper lesson about obedience. Isn't that how God works? You think that you have learned all there is to know about something, and He pulls the rug right out from underneath you to show you that you don't.

I already knew how to be obedient to the Lord. When God said to move in a certain way, I started walking. When God said to stand still and wait for Him, I was still. When God said to speak, I spoke only what I felt that He wanted me to say. I had already learned it all. Or so I thought. It's amazing...just when you think that you have learned all you can learn about God, He comes in only to prove you know nothing. As a Christian, I had heard all the stories about Shadrach, Meshach, and Abednego. I had read all the amazing feats of courage and faith that the saints had to overcome to glorify God. But to me, that's all they were—stories of crazy acts of heroism that didn't happen anymore.

However, every day since my surgery, when I woke up on that surgery table and I knew that something had changed, God has been telling me more about the small stepping stones of these heroes. Every hero has to learn about this stone, and we don't always understand the need for it. But this stone is in everyone's story. Because without it, we can't truly become a follower of Christ.

Obedience.

The simple act of obedience is a human's hardest obstacle. It is every sinner's downfall. The fallen one, himself, could not submit to God and trust that He knew best. His pride and arrogance got him kicked out of Heaven after leading a bunch of God's Children in a rebellion against God. Adam and Eve disobeyed God by eating the fruit of the Tree of Knowledge of Good and Evil. (Genesis 2:16) God's People made idols and worshiped them, disobeying God. (Exodus 32) I could go through the Bible and tell of a thousand more acts of disobedience against God, but then I would miss my point entirely.

My point is that there were great heroes who glorified God and elevated themselves to a higher station by obeying God. Those who learn to obey and listen to God gain favor, wisdom, and honor in God's Eyes. Queen Esther obeyed her uncle, Mordecai. She followed her family's traditions but respected her king's rule, which gave her favor and love from her king. (Read the whole book of Esther in the Bible. You won't regret it.)

Noah listened to God and started building a huge boat. God told him to make it out of Cypress wood and pitch. God gave him the dimensions with explicit instructions as to who would accompany him on this boat. When you read Genesis 6, you don't read about the times that Noah lived in, but you do hear about God's Judgment of the creation He had made. God was, for lack of better words, disgusted by the life that people were living. God tells us in the scriptures that the sons of God found God's creation (woman) to be beautiful, and so they came down and married any of them that they chose. I would love to say that's what happened, but I get this feeling their "love" of women was on the wrong side of honor because God saw man's wicked heart and the lust that ran through them. God condemns the world to death and orders the Earth to be flooded. The only family God granted sanctuary to was Noah, his wife, his sons, and their wives.

When the water poured out of the Heavens and up from the crevices of the Earth for forty days and nights. However, what everyone seems to overlook is that they were not just on that boat for forty days and forty nights. The rain stopped coming down after forty days and forty nights, but God sustained the flooded waters on the Earth for one hundred and fifty days. I could not imagine how horrible the sounds were during the flood. How hard it could have been to listen to the people begging for help. The screaming and yelling that came at Noah and his family for not helping them. I know the scriptures tell us that God ordered them to enter the boat and that God shut the doors behind them, but I couldn't imagine that the boat was soundproof. You know? I can only pray that God had given Noah and his family mercy and grace. Hopefully, they were spared the agony of having to hear the remaining sounds of a dying generation. Hopefully, because of their obedience, He was still a good God who loved them. But then after the sounds of the water pouring in, the sounds of the people crying for help, the sounds of the other animals dying…Comes the silence. The sounds of the water crashing against the sides of the boat. The monotonous daily boredom. It had to have been hard. But Noah and his family were heroes despite the hard things they had to live through.

~ * ~

David despite the hard things he had to live through was

God's Hero. Despite Jesse's disdain for him, David listened to his father and tended to the sheep in the fields. We don't have much in scripture that tells us about David's life growing up, and I might be taking creative liberties to assume this, but I couldn't imagine that David had a mentor to teach him how to kill the lion or to teach him to face a bear. But He had God showing him in the fields how to take on the enemies. Scripture tells us that after ten generations, God was speaking to David, and David listened. Growing up, I have heard God speak to me. I heard and felt His Presence guiding me. God was there in every situation telling me how to remain safe. Leading me where to go. I could see my choices laid before me. I could not imagine that David's life was any different. I could not imagine that your life is any different than ours.

If you learn to take the time to stop and listen. I know, I know. I can hear your objections and excuses from here. I can hear the "I don't know how to hear Him" or the "He doesn't speak to me like the way He speaks to you" excuses. I have heard them over and over in my counsel to others. If you have accepted Jesus Christ as your Lord and Savior, then the Holy Spirit entered your mind and body when you asked Him to. God is there, living in you. Breathing in your lungs, living in your heart. He is speaking all day, every day. He never goes away. He never leaves you and will never forsake you. He is always with you. At first, He is loud and clear when you are first saved because His Voice is new and invigorating. Your mind and body are aligned with Him, and everything you see and hear is drenched in His Presence. The world and the stresses it carries have faded away. But it has to come back eventually.

Many hear Him call them to Himself to be saved, but they never know where to go after that. They keep going to church because they feel that is what they are supposed to do. Which it is, don't get me wrong, but that isn't your finish line. God tells us that some live in this world, and when the gospel of truth is preached, the seeds are thrown out on the soil. The soil is a person's heart and mind. There are some that the soil is soft, fertile, and ready for God's Seeds to be planted in their hearts. It grows, matures, and begins to take root in their heart. The seed, if cared for and tended to, can grow into a tree of life within us and produce fruit for others to eat and be nourished by. As can anything we see, hear, or touch. That's why we are to renew our minds in the Word of God daily. So that we can never become hardened or dry.

We need God's Living Water to flow through us to keep our hearts washed from the dirt of life. If we are not paying attention to our surroundings and the people that are around us, then we can find ourselves walking off our righteous path. We won't even know it's happening. Before we know it, we can find ourselves doing and saying things for all the wrong reasons. In my observations and experiences, we can usually find them selfishly motivated. We thought we were doing it for the right reason. In our minds, it sounded legitimate. But when we looked at the fruits of what we had produced, it was all wrong.

Selfishness…

I believe it is the reason for all sin. They say that the root of all evil is money, but I think it goes much deeper than that. Money cannot do anything. No more than we can blame a murder on a gun. It all comes from the heart, but isn't that what God tells us?

In Matthew 15:19, he tells us, *"For out of the heart proceed evil thoughts, murders, adulteries, fornications, thefts, false witness, blasphemies."*

So if we carry the seeds of all our actions in our hearts, then shouldn't we be guarding it better? Shouldn't we be more careful about what comes into our eyes, ears, and what touches our bodies? We shouldn't want to watch movies or commercials that display unGodly, unhealthy activities. We shouldn't want to listen to music that speaks of a lifestyle that doesn't agree with the way that God tells us is the way HE wants us to live. Before you get defensive and say you can't live like that or listen to that type of music...do some research first. Better yet, reach out to me. Because I can point you to artists that can throw down in a rap battle with any street artist, and guess what...They are praising the name of Jesus Christ. Rare of Breed, Joe Nester, and LeCrae, to name a few. If it's about the lifestyle... Then that's a different issue entirely.

However, it brings me back to obedience. The things in your life that you can't let go of, the things that you day make you who you are, and that you are clinging so desperately to...Why? Why do they define you? Who do they say you are? What do they say you're made of? Let me guess...the music. It says you are good at spitting out words that make you more powerful than the other guy on the other corner. The drugs...oh, it says you can't live without them. That you have to have it because you can't function in this life without it. The friends...they say they will die with you or for you. Or that they have your back no matter what. That they will be there with you and will never leave you. Oh, I see. It's all about the money, right? It gives you the power to get, give, and control everything in your life. Do you hear the theme playing out here? All these things say you can't live, breathe, or go on without them. These are called addictions, and that, my friend, is a disability.

The definition of a disability is a physical or mental condition that limits a person's movements, senses, or activities. That's not freedom. That is bondage, and the sad thing is that the enemy has you believing you're in control of it. When in reality, it has control of everything you say and do. You are a slave to it. You won't be satisfied until you drink it, smoke it, or consume it. You can't be whole until you wear it, spend it, or show others that you have it. Your livelihood depends on obtaining possession of these things. Until you get them, your life is not worth living.

My Friend, joy and happiness are free. Free to us like the air that we breathe in every day. If you can't get happy unless you have something else on Earth, then it has control over you. You have made that thing an idol in your life. You have said that these things can do something for you that you cannot do for yourself. Which leads me to idolatry. Idolatry is the extreme love or admiration for something or someone.

When God delivered His People from Egypt, He told Moses that they would be His Special Treasure. That they were His People above all other people. That they would be a Holy Nation of Priests. He was on Mount Sinai with Moses, and He gave Moses the commandments for God's People to live by. Through these commandments, His People would remain a Holy Nation. I know your mind went straight to your Sunday school class where we all learned of the Ten Commandments, but in reality, God gave Moses six hundred and thirteen commandments for His People to be guided and led by. These commandments spoke to everything in someone's life. Everything from daily hygiene to the foods that they could eat. From the clothes they were allowed to wear to the jewelry, their women adorned themselves with. God had specific instructions for His People to be guided by to keep them holy. God was not playing around. He meant business.

Just breathe. I am not going to tell you that you have to adapt to the six hundred and thirteen commandments that God gave Moses. When God gave us Jesus Christ and He died to save us from those sins, He came to fulfill the law of Moses. His Death gave us grace. Romans 6 explains it to us. Galatians 2 & 3 tells us even more about it. Nonetheless, because of Jesus Christ, we can now be free from the slavery of sin. We still have commandments to live by. We have the Bible that gives us many testimonials of rules to guide us and to live by. These lessons have worked for generations of believers to live a better life than one filled with pain and suffering. So why would we continue to live a life of bondage and be a slave to things that wish us harm and death? Why would we want to hold onto friends who lie, cheat, and abandon us in our times of need? It makes no sense to crave things that hurt us when there is a way we can be free of them. If your lifestyle keeps you in bondage, then why would you want to stay that way? Don't you want to be happy? Free to live a life that allows you to smile, have friends, and travel? Just saying...

By obeying God's Commandments, we are given the way, the truth, and the life free of sin. Free of a life being scared of nine-foot-tall giants who want to kill us and all our family for our beliefs. David stood before Goliath, having overcome his inability to listen to God's Law. Shoot. As we learned in the last chapter, his family had ten generations of God's Law to learn from. I didn't go through the generations of lessons because I was afraid that by doing so, I would miss the point that I am trying to make to you. Which is we all have to learn the lesson that it's better to be obedient to God and follow after Him than to go after things that cause us harm, maybe even death. No one is glorified by mastering the art of death. There are no rewards to be received in hell. The devil doesn't tell us that if we follow him we'll be rewarded for doing so.

However, God does. God tells us that if we follow Him and obey His Commandments, we will be rewarded with life after death. (Colossians 3:23, Matthew 16:27, 2 Timothy 4:8) In my experiences, I have found that the rewards of listening to God can be felt here on Earth before we die as well. The freedom we receive from the bondage alcohol or drugs have on us is a great reward. I have seen relationships restored. Marriages that were broken and damaged, be healed and renewed. I have witnessed amazing things because of the work Jesus Christ has done in a person's mind and heart. I have heard of hope restored, joy renewed, and love rekindled. There is nothing you could tell me about the greatness of Heaven that could compare to the miracles I have seen in my life. There is only one thing greater—and that is seeing the glorified face of my Jesus Christ. My Lord and Savior, who died on the cross to save me from my sins. He and He alone is worthy of all my praise. There is no greater reward for me. To see Him ride out of the Heavens on His White Horse and His Banner flying high on the flags of those who follow Him into battle. Oh Hallelujah!!

David stood on that field of battle, in front of a nasty Goliath, ready for whatever he was going to face. He had already learned his lesson of obedience. He had already learned that heeding God's Words in the battle to go left or right exactly when God told him to, would give him the advantage over any opponent. He stood there knowing that

God would take care of him. That no matter what happened, he was in God's hands. That God would bring him through it all. There were a few moments in my life when I felt God speak so loud that I could have sworn He was standing right next to me, telling me what to do. Throughout the scriptures, we are told that God's followers called for His Help and He answered them.

So why would we think David's experiences there, standing in front of Goliath, were any different? How could David stand in front of King Saul and say I'll fight this uncircumcised Philistine and take him down. He is no match for the Lord Almighty! Scripture tells us that Goliath came out of his tent and screamed obscenities at the Israelite people. To cause them to fear and torment them with his height—his strength. Puffing out his chest and slamming his sword into his shield to make them jump in fear. He did this for forty days before the day of battle. He'd come out in the morning and make his spectacle, and in the evening, before they went to sleep. The scriptures also tell us that when God removed His Favor from Saul He allowed a spirit to torment Saul's mind. So Saul was already in distress. So when he went out to litigate the battle, we can only imagine that he was weak and terrified. But there in Saul's tent stood David, a young man who played the lyre (a guitar) for King Saul to calm him down when he was tormented by the evil spirit. David wasn't huge in stature. He wasn't rough and hairy, full of war wisdom and experience. By the world's standards, David was a nobody. A young man full of charisma and youth.

There he stood in Saul's tent proclaiming that no one should be allowed to stand there and defy the Lord their God. Especially a Philistine such as Goliath. That no man should be so arrogant and foolish as to mock the authority of

God. David, little righteous David, standing before a king, demanding it be stopped. When King Saul says it can't be done and that David doesn't know what he is talking about, David gets upset at him. He knows the authority of who God is. He has seen God act in his own life, and I imagine that upsets David even more. I can hear David as he tells Saul that God delivered him from a lion and a bear—that if Saul would send David out to fight this Philistine, then God would deliver him from death there too! I can hear the confidence in David's voice now!

As the memories of the huge lion's paw almost clutching David's throat pass through his mind. As the growl of the bear tries to torment David into submission; but fails. I can feel David's fists clench as he screams, "Who is this uncircumcised Philistine who defies the Lord, My God?" Who does this idiot think he is? It would be as if I, coming in at five feet, two inches tall, were standing in front of Shaquille O'Neal, who is standing on a two-foot-tall box! Only he is screaming and yelling ugly, hateful things across the field at me. Or better yet…any stereotypical unbeliever standing across the street. Yelling obscene, derogatory things about me because I have a bumper sticker that says I was a Christian. Or a co-worker across the break room who sees me praying over my food.

Now I am not saying we need to get our slingshots and rocks and take them out, but we can stand in front of those who do not understand us and, with confidence, tell them exactly why we know God loves us. Or why God loves them? We know these things, just as little David did. We have scary people every day who try to get us to back down from what we believe. To shame us into running away from the fight and getting as far as we can from the blood, gore, and guts of the war. We stand in front of a despicable enemy who will do whatever they can to disgrace us and make our testimony unworthy of God's Name. We have a pagan caught up in sexual conflict, addicted drug users, abusive alcoholic men, and hungry activists who crave attention, hashtags, and bonuses. Who will stop at nothing to achieve front-page news in a mediocre pyramid of chaos? We all have family members who defy the love and law of God. Who, at every family get-together, mock and look down on us for what we believe in. For who we believe in. They look at us like we are poor, uneducated, weak members of society who have been tricked into believing in nonsense that has no purpose in our lives today.

As Christians, we are called to act, live, and respond with a better attitude than the ones they are dishing out. God says that we should not fight these battles the way they fight, but show them there is a better way to live. We have to show them that even though the world is hard and comes at us with a vengeance, we can still be holy and happy at the same time. We are called to show them that despite the evil that stands before us we can stand with honor, righteousness, and power. That our blessings aren't found in mountains of money or wealth. That we are stronger, faster, and more passionate than our enemies. So that when the time comes and the world around them is falling apart and they don't know what to do, they remember that we were in the very same position as they are now in and we did not crumble. Because if we can't show them that, then what did Jesus die on the cross for? I'm pretty sure it wasn't my witty demeanor or my quick replies. I know Jesus didn't die for my fleshly, negative outlook that I have about the human population or my quick ability to judge someone.

I think that when Jesus was dying for me on that cross that day, He saw the best version of me that I could possibly be. You know the one who is beautiful, inside and out. The one who can look past someone's bad days and still see goodness and sunshine. He saw a mother who was calm and patient as she taught her child how to tie their shoe. Or remained firm but told them the hundredth time to get that room cleaned up before they went out to play with the neighborhood kids. He saw an aunt who was there and always willing to help. He saw someone who could be the person her family could call on for prayers and advice. He knew a wife who was loving and supportive of her husband as he provided for their home and family. A helper and someone who would get things done for him that he couldn't do for himself. I would hate to think that the only thing Jesus saw that day on that cross was a Pharisee screaming obscenities at Him as He died. I hope that He saw me living my best life, strong in His Sacrifice. That's who I hope Jesus saw that day. How about you? Who do you think Jesus saw when He died for your sins that day?

~ * ~

So if Jesus died on the cross to erase all the bad that we have done in our lives, then why do we make it so hard to become that person now? Even after we are saved? Jesus wasn't born, I think, for another twelve generations after David, but I would be naive if I thought that Jesus didn't die for David's soul as well. As a matter of fact, I know that He did. Jesus did not come to abolish the law but to fulfill it. All of Jesus' forefathers paved the way for His Coming and His Death. Everything that they did in their lifetimes made the way for Jesus to come to us in the flesh. It tells us in the scriptures that the Word is God, the Word was God, and it came to life in Jesus Christ. God came to us in human form to die for our sins. He gave Himself because He loved us so much.

John 3:16 says, *"For God loved the world so much, that He gave His only begotten son, that whosoever believes in Him shall not perish but have eternal life."*

It doesn't tell us that He only loved the people who got up and went to church every Sunday like good little followers. He doesn't tell us that He only loved white people, black people, or people without tattoos. He didn't just forgive the simple sinners who never hurt anyone else. No, God loved us ALL! He loved the tattooed killers as much as He loved the little white girl who sits wide-eyed in awe in church on Sunday morning. He loves the sinners who keep falling away and running from Him as much as He does the preacher. He loves the poor, dirty, uneducated sinners as much as He loves you and me. He loved us all! You see, we are all called to Him. We are all called to come home.

There is nothing in my mind or spirit that tells me that David was not called to the battlefield that day. Of course, Jesse told him to go there with food for his brothers, but I feel that in his spirit, he thought that he was supposed to be there. Everything that had happened to David in his life up to now had led him to be in King Saul's tent advising him on that day of battle. He had already learned how to hear God's Voice. He had already learned the lessons that guided him to kill the lion and the bear. He had already learned the calling of God's Voice telling him to go where God was telling him to go...But wait. His father may have told him to go to the front lines of the battlefield to deliver food to his brothers, but where do we read that God told him to step in and be the warrior to defeat the Philistines tormenting the Israelites?

There is a big difference between being called to go somewhere to deliver food and then being told to kill a 9-foot-9-inch giant and chop off his head with his sword. But as I read and reread the account of that day, my spirit kept showing me the doubt of everyone around David. Over and over, the scriptures tell us that no one believed in David. That he was a useless nobody who tended to the sheep in the fields. The men in the camp, the warrior even rolled their eyes and turned their backs to him because they knew this little boy did not know what he was talking about. David's chest was all puffed up, being arrogant in his words. Trying to look like he was an equal to them. Like he knew what the blood of battle felt like as he took the life of another man. His brothers even asked him why he was there and asked him why he had left the sheep unattended. As if to say, he was going to upset his father again for leaving them defenseless. Even his friend King Saul told him, "You are a young boy and have business here in battle. What will you do, play the lyre and sing him to sleep?" I'm being a little dramatic there, but I can only imagine the ridicule David was getting.

However, maybe his tone was what was getting him the wrong kind of attention. Maybe he hadn't learned to walk in the authority that God was laying on him yet. The lessons that he had been through taught him that he had the strength to overcome great obstacles, therefore giving him a big ego. But his reputation with his peers had not yet caught on. In his mind and heart, David knew God had made him to accomplish great things, but the world was not aware of him yet. He was called to be a great king and to bring the Israelite people back into great fortune, but those were the only things he could feel. It wasn't until he stood before Goliath that he knew that he had stepped out of his calling and was beginning to walk the calling out into the world. Who knows, maybe he still wasn't aware of his greatness at that time.

Thomas Edison failed to invent the light bulb over a thousand times. He had the idea, then he began research and development. From the beginning of his concept till its final working model, Edison had spent two whole years bringing the idea to light. That was only the start of his journey. He then had to work on production, find usable materials, and source the project for manufacturing for the world to utilize.

Greatness takes TIME! When it comes to learning, understanding, and reflecting on all there is to know about God, we can say this with full assurance. We will NEVER reach the end of fully knowing all God knows. We can only keep seeking His Face and Wisdom to overcome what we can in our lifetime. That was one thing that Lucifer, satan, could never understand. Even after all he knew and the time he had spent with God, he was still not going to be Him. He could never overthrow Him. He would never be more powerful than Him. In satan's pride and arrogance, he allowed himself to be deceived that he was greater than God. It can never be done. Trust me, many angels have fallen from their place in Heaven, thinking they were better than He, only to find out they were wrong.

You see, Morningstar (That was satan's name in Heaven) was called to be an archangel. He was a high-ranking angel when he was serving the Lord. Scriptures don't give us a specific account of his job in Heaven. However, there were several mentions throughout the Bible that tell us a little about who he was to God before he fell. His name means Light Bringer. I believe names are of great importance to God. He tells us in the scriptures that every star has a name to Him and He knows their names. He made sure Adam and He sat down and gave every living creature a name. Several times in the Bible, God even went ahead and changed people's names to reflect a great monument of change in their lives. Abram's name was changed to Abraham. (Genesis 17:5) Sarai's name was changed to Sarah. (Genesis 17:15) Jacob's name was changed to Israel. (Genesis 32:22) God tells us in Revelation 2:17 that when He is talking to the churches, He tells them that He will give them their new name. No one knows it except those who receive it.

I think that in our minds and hearts, we can feel the greatness that God is calling us to. The closer our relationship gets with Him, the more we will understand what he is saying to us and what He expects from us. You have to spend more time with Him. Listening to Him. Calling on Him and asking Him for His Opinion. That means you need to set aside time in your day to do that. You schedule time to get your oil changed. To get your hair cut. To make money and to talk to your mother. Is it not more important to schedule time for you to sit and talk with God?

Look at people in scripture. Job spent time with the Lord every morning and made sacrifices to Him just in case his children had sinned. (Job 1:1) Daniel prayed and fasted before the Lord when King Nebuchadnezzar took over Judah. (Daniel 1:1) Mordecai prayed and fasted before the Lord when Esther went before her king. (Esther 4) Even Jesus spent a lot of time talking to God in His Quiet time when He wasn't ministering to people. We are not exempt from this. God needs us to spend time with Him. How are we to know His Heart and be able to minister to others about Him, if we do not know Him? We would have nothing to testify about. We would only be guessing and making it up. We would be assuming that what God wants us to do and say is the truth, but we would not know for sure. In the end, we would be called a false prophet or a false teacher. I believe the world already has an abundance of these on hand. So we do not need to add to the hurt and pain the church could be causing the world. What the world needs right now is the truth.

There have already been so many who felt the Holy Spirit move in themselves and have demanded a microphone to speak to the nations. When in reality, the Lord was speaking just to them. There is a big difference between a Word from God that needs to be spoken to a body of believers to edify them and a word for an individual. I have seen and heard words that were spoken from a pulpit that were meant for a single person, and the pastor was in such a hurry to deliver the word, that they spoke it over the whole church. Every sick person in the room jumps up to receive that healing and everyone who heard the word claims it for someone else they know. People then make life decisions that they shouldn't have because someone else convinced them that God was healing them. Those are dangerous assumptions to make about the Words that the Lord gives.

So, please, be respectful of the calling God has placed on your life. If you hear something in your spirit and you're not sure what to do with it or about it, then write it down with a date set it to the side, and pray over it. WAIT ON GOD to tell you where to go with it. If there is any lesson that I have learned over time, it is that whatever the enemy can't stop, he will accelerate. So, again, time is your best friend. I have felt God say something to me before about a specific person on a specific matter but wasn't sure when I would ever get to speak to them about what I had heard. So I wrote down their names, the date with the time, and I waited for God to tell me when to go. Actually, I never got told to go because a day later, God brought them to me! If I had rushed to them about what I was hearing, they wouldn't have been ready to hear what God needed them to hear. I would've gone in there in a hurry and confused the heck out of them. But since I had waited on God, I was in His Timing, and what do they always say about God's Timing? God's Timing is always perfect. The Word was delivered and received in good soil that was ready to accept it to move forward.

God doesn't need us to plan anything for Him. He needs us to trust Him and to listen to Him. He needs us to obey. So when we are released to do and say things to others, we can do it effectively. His ways are higher than our ways. We may never understand the impact that our obedience has. But I can tell you this, not being obedient to the Lord will push people further away from Him. Your lying, gossiping, and your bad temper will hurt others to the point you will lose them. God tells us in scripture that if we lie, then we are like our father, satan. Because he is the father of lies, and that's not where I want to be when I die.

There are also times when God will not need us to do anything or say anything at all. There was a huge part of my walk where I was supposed to be still and just stand. I spent many years upset with God because I was on fire for Him in my heart and soul, and I wanted Him to use me. I had no voice, but I wanted to speak. I wanted to testify, but I had no testimony. I wanted to serve, but there was no one else in the room. All He kept saying to me was to stand still. For years, I stood there. Watching the world fly by as I remained still. I got to see others promoted in the church, while I sat there, invisible. After a while, I realized that if God was going to use me one day, then I had to be ready. I had to learn all that I could so that I would be effective in my Kingdom Work.

That's when I started to learn how to serve the church and the church body. I think I could write a whole other book entirely when I begin thinking about all that goes into running a church. Physically, mentally, spiritually—it's all exhausting if you think about it from a human perspective. To be honest with you, I think that is why kings only reign for a small part of their lives. It's overwhelming to think about all the things that go into running a castle or a kingdom. There are so many people involved in running a kingdom, but there is only one steadfast rule. There is a king and you are not him. You are there to live, breathe, and serve at the request of your king.

Whereas the church, our king, was also our servant. In our human strength, we alone cannot keep the church moving forward. It is a full-time job just to pastor a church. Don't even get me started on the hours it takes to maintain and clean the building, keep the sound and stage running effectively, and keep the grounds cut, mulched, and looking good. There are not enough volunteers to make it happen effectively. Not in their human strength. If you are serving the church to gain the glory of men, then that is all you will receive. But if you are working to serve the Lord God with your gifts, then you're in the right place.

Serving the church has shown me so much about God's Heart. The perseverance required when serving the church is a heavy responsibility for anyone. In our physical form, we are never enough. In our minds, we are not smart enough. In our spirit, we are not strong enough. We do not have enough degrees to teach any one specific individual how to effectively run a church to preach the gospel. Because if God isn't in it, then what is the point? Without God, in time, you will get burned out. You'll run out of things to say. You will have reached the peak of all you know. You will run out of lessons, songs, and sermons. Without God guiding you, you will fall out of the race. He is your source for all things. If God has called you to it, then He will have made you to do it. A preacher will be an untapped well of messages that he could speak. A children's pastor will be a source of ways to reach children about God. A youth pastor will be an untapped source for all things cool to young adults hungry for God. A worship leader will thrive on making music for the Lord. A church greeter will always be outgoing and friendly as unto the Lord. If God gifted them to serve the church, then HE made them and equipped them to be the church.

If God is calling you to it, then it's up to you to obey. Otherwise, you're doing it for yourself. I think David had to learn this to be able to pick up his second stone to place in his bag. If he had never learned to hear God's Voice, then he would have never known which direction God wanted him to walk. Without God's Voice, he would have never known what to say. If he hadn't learned from the experiences of the lessons that God was teaching him, he wouldn't have been able to be confident in his words to King Saul. Then, without his confidence in God who was with him, he would have never been able to walk before Goliath and slay him with a slingshot and a stone. David had to overcome these lessons to effectively overthrow Goliath that day. In my vision, I can feel David breathe out as he remembers all his lessons about obedience. I can feel him release the weakness of his strength and as it leaves him, he inhales the newness of God's Strength as it pours into his body. His obedience to God gave him the strength to do as he was called to do. Without Fear.

Chapter Three: Fear

3

In the New King James Bible, God addresses fear over five hundred times. He speaks to us in parables, riddles, and even in plain verse. Directing and carefully guiding us away from the person we used to be before HE came into our lives. There is nothing on Earth that we should be afraid of. No man. No animal. No debt. No demon or spirit. There is only one thing HE does tell us to be afraid of. He said in Proverbs 1:7,

"The fear of the Lord is the beginning of knowledge."

Ecclesiastes 12:13 says, *"Fear God and keep His Commandments."*

As we get closer to God, we begin to understand who He is and what He wants from us. However, we cannot learn about Him unless we look into the past and who He is and has always been. We cannot understand who He is now if we don't look into the past and understand Him then. We would be naive and ill-informed if we thought that the God who is written in the Bible is not the same God who lives today. He is the same as He was yesterday. If you think He is not, then you are sadly mistaken. The same things He hated and would not forgive in the past are the same things He hates today. There is only one reason why He has not struck many of our towns down like He did with Sodom and Gomorrah. Right now we are living in Grace. We are living in a time covered in Jesus' Grace. (Galatians 3:13)

When Jesus died on the cross for our sins, then rose to sit at the right hand of God (Matthew 26:64), He left us with a grace that would cover us from God's Judgment till He came back for us. (2 Thessalonians 2) (Romans 1:18-32; 2 Peter 3:9) Numerous scriptures speak about the grace we now live in, but it does not absolve us of sin. Not until we repent and change from our sinful ways. Then accept Jesus Christ as our Lord and Savior who died for those sins. However, the burden of faith becomes even heavier because we now know the truth. We know that we should not do those sinful things that God says are wrong, and if we do them anyway, then there is no sacrifice available to us. (Hebrews 10:26-27) He tells us here,

"We can be certain of fearful judgment, and a fiery indignation which will devour the enemies of God."

So whom shall I fear?

So there is no one greater to fear than the Lord...I wish I could wholeheartedly say that there is nothing on Earth that I am afraid of, and I will save you the long list of things that freak me out. I am afraid of things that are out there and could end my life. But I do not stand paralyzed in fear. I take them to the Lord daily, because without Him, I am a lost little sheep away from my pack. However, I must be honest with you, I have faced some great trials in my life, and no matter how difficult they were, I was able to stand strong and not give in to weakness.   The only reason I was able to stand so confidently was not because I knew what was going to happen or whether or not things were going to go my way. I was able to stand because I knew who held my future in His Hand. I knew God was there with me. I knew that whatever the outcome was, I would be okay and able to make it tomorrow. I had already lived through some of the worst days of my life so far, and God held me up through it all.

So what were the fears that David had to overcome to be so confident as he picked up that third stone? Some of them we have already researched and uncovered in the scriptures. He was an outcast in his Israeli community because of the curse placed on his family line ten generations before his birth in the incident of Judah and Tamar. We learned that his father was hoping to have intimate relations with his wife's maid and was tricked into having relations with his wife instead. We can assume his father looked down on David for his mother's actions from the journal left behind by the maid in the Jewish People Museum. We can assume he was afraid of the rejection of his father. His father raised him to tend to the sheep, instead of being a warrior like his older brothers. Given his actions and loud mouth on the day he faced Goliath, we can assume that he wanted to be a warrior like them because he was excited and ran to the front lines to his brothers to see the action.

He had to overcome his fear of death from a lion and a bear in the fields while he was tending the sheep...that would have been scary enough. However, there was one issue we hadn't discussed yet about what David was facing in his day. We read in scripture about Saul disobeying the Lord when he went and fought against the Amalekites. We learned that after that, Samuel was told by God to go to Jesse's house because that was where he was going to find the new king that God wanted to replace Saul. If you had read the remaining part of that story, you would've read that Samuel anointed David with Holy Oil to consecrate God's Choice over his life. He was anointed David in front of his father and his brothers. What scripture doesn't tell us is what happened after that day and the details that transpired between the time God chose him to the time he went to the front lines to face Goliath.

The very next portion of reading in scripture, the Bible tells us about the tormenting spirit sent by the Lord to trouble Saul. I struggled with this for quite some time because the Word says that the Spirit was sent to trouble Saul from God. I never really saw God as one who would cause us harm, and if I am being honest with you, I am still trying to understand it myself. But if we have read anything in the Bible at all, we have to know that God does cause harm to those who are against Him. I keep trying to reason with the idea in my head, that maybe God didn't command the spirit to torment him, that He merely removed His Presence or favor that was upon Saul, and when He removed his protection from Saul, the evil spirits came upon him.

If we look closer in the scriptures we can find that there are other situations in scripture where we see a person was possessed or tormented by an evil spirit. Like in the life of Mary (called Magdalene), who was tormented by seven demons when Jesus cast them out of her. (Luke 8:2) Eliphaz the Temanite, a friend of Job's, was telling him about an encounter he had with something in the night that scared him. He says to Job that a spirit brushed past his face and the hair on his body stood up. (Job 4) There was a boy and his father who came before Jesus. The boy's father explained to Jesus that the young boy had a deaf and mute spirit come on him. He said that there were some times when the spirit seized the boy, it would try to throw him into fire or water to kill him. Jesus cast the spirit out and told them that anyone who truly believes and through prayer can do this. (Mark 9:14) But there aren't many times where God was the deliverer of the evil spirit upon someone's life. I did find a few times when God commanded it to come to pass. In the story of Abimelech and the leaders of Shechem, God sends an evil spirit to stir up trouble between them. (Judges 9:23) God has also claimed that He made good, but when He made good, evil was born. (Isaiah 45:7)

Maybe Saul's genes and DNA had a mental illness already activated in him, and when God's Presence left him, his genetics reverted to what his life should have been before God made him king. But I cannot deny the scriptures. It clearly states that the spirit was sent by God to torment him, and so I have to believe it as it is written. So there Saul is tormented by a spirit distressed, and fighting to be king when God removed His Favor from him. He was being tormented by this spirit, and it says that his servants suggest to him that maybe he should call someone to play the lyre and sing to him. That might help calm him down and provide him relief. They suggest that there is a young son of Jesse's who plays and sings with the lyre and that the king should call for him. They tell the king that David is favored to play for the Lord. So King Saul knew that God had blessed him. That persuaded the king to call for him. He could no longer get Samuel to come to him, so he did whatever he could for relief.

He had already pleaded with Samuel his excuses for his disobedience. He humbly described to Samuel that he was afraid of his men, and that is why he let them take the property and Amalekites king. But it didn't matter to God— He was upset with Saul for his disobedience, and just like that, God was done with him. I don't know about you, but that would upset me as a king. Hey, I'm human too. Could you, in all your wealth and power, just walk away because of a little mistake? It would be hard! Shoot, we get upset when we get a ticket and have to go to court to pay a fine. How much more upset would you be if you were king and your prophet told you that your time as king was done because you didn't obey? He was king. He shouldn't have to listen to this...Yeah, I am being creative here, but we have to understand the emotion that Saul and David were feeling. Because we, too, are human and we fail God too. So what does Saul do then? He does what any king going through that would do. He orders his spies to keep tabs on Samuel. Saul knows that God told him to appoint another in Saul's place. So he has to get to him before Samuel can appoint him.

Scripture tells us that the elders of Bethlehem trembled at Samuel's coming. They wanted to know if this prophet and servant of God was coming to them in peace or to bring them harm. They were afraid because they were not sure why he was there. They did not know that God had sent him on a mission to Jesse's house to find a king. I would find it hard to believe that they had heard yet that God was replacing Saul. They didn't have the internet or phones yet. So the news back then was either sent by messenger (a written note on paper, sealed, and then delivered by a person...not online through Facebook) Even then the news that was shared was news that the king approved of being sent out and I would find it naive of me to think he would want the kingdom to know that God did not want him to be their king anymore.

Most kings back then did horrible things to the children of

a defeated ruler and families of previous rulers because they did not want there to be a legitimate heir to the throne that could claim the throne in the future and come to take it back. So if they won a battle and overtook your kingdom, they would kill you, your children, and your wives so that no one could rally an army to come and fight on your behalf to get your kingdom back. So I would imagine that Saul's counsel and advisory boards were all telling him to seek this new king out and have him killed. That way, he wouldn't have the claim that God wanted him to be their king.

The fear that was assumed had to be enough to worry Samuel and Jesse. Once David was anointed before his father and his brothers, it had to be a family secret until God saw fit to bring him into his reign. Could you only imagine the fear they were going through when Saul's servants called Jesse to allow David to be brought to the palace to play his lyre and to sing to the king? Jesse went from being disgraced and an outcast in his community to being the father of a soon-to-be crowned king from God. Even if this was only playing out in his mind and no one else in the community knew what was going on, Jesse still had received some life-altering news. He was a shepherd. He was not a man of riches and glory. He probably worked and clawed for everything he had, and it still wasn't a lot. He, we assume, didn't even like David. He didn't even see him as worthy of recognition or a chance to be chosen when he stood next to his other sons.

Could you imagine the look on Jesse's face when Samuel says God has chosen David to be king? Then anoints and consecrates him with the oil from his horn? He doesn't just take a dab of oil from his flask to mark his forehead like he did with Saul. Samuel pours the oil from the horn over David's head! Can you just see that play out in your mind?

Jesse and his other son's mouths hanging wide open, looking at each other like this has got to be a joke! Are we being punked here? Looking around for a mastermind who was playing a huge joke on them all for laughs. This little spindly sheepherder, a king?!? Then looking over at humble David with dark curls popping up from the oil as he geeks with pride and honor. Then they all get worried as David stood there, unaware of the danger he had just been put in.

You see, David's three oldest brothers served in high ranks in King Saul's Army. So they would've known right away what Saul's reaction was going to be when hearing this. I am sure that they were all worried. However, scripture never tells us that they lived or played that fear out. Jesse never stopped David from going before King Saul because he was afraid for his son's life. He didn't pack a bag for David and tell him to run from the king because he would be killed. Everything went along as if nothing had changed in their lives. So either they were all pretending they weren't afraid and that they knew nothing, or Jesse and his sons didn't believe that God really had chosen David to become the king. Or maybe Jesse truly didn't love David because of his mother's deceitfulness. Who knows maybe he thought it was a blessing that Saul was calling for David. Saul would kill David and he wouldn't be held accountable for him any longer. Either way, David went to King Saul to play him a song on his lyre.

As he played for King Saul, he found favor with the king through God's Presence in him. You're a Christian! You know how that goes. God's Presence that lives in you pushes evil away from you. I have had people tell me that when they are in my house, they feel so safe and calm. I have had others who are capable of seeing and sensing evil spirits come to my home and tell me that there are thousands of evil spirits and demons screaming and being tormented at my property line. They are angry and upset that they can't get to my home to hurt us. You see, when we walk, talk, and spend time with the Lord, we carry Him with us everywhere we go. Like the scriptures tell us—Grace and Mercy shall follow us all the days of our lives. He tells us that He goes before us to make a way for us. He walks with us hand in hand. That He protects us and keeps us from harm.

So I think that David knew that when he went before the king. He felt God was with him and that no harm would come to him. Whether he consciously knew it or if he had no clue, God was there with him. God's Presence in David calmed the tormenting spirit and brought King Saul peace. Therefore, making David an instant friend to the king. David still lived and worked for his father, but when the king was overwhelmed by the spirit, he called on David, like a sick patient who would call on a doctor for healing. David did not live with the king full-time. So when David was sent to the front lines with supplies and food for his brothers, he was already somewhat familiar with the people he was with. Some would say too familiar by the way he was running off at the mouth, the way that he was.

Even when he got in front of King Saul, he said with confidence that Goliath was a nobody the king needed to worry about. Because of the way scripture describes the story, I imagine King Saul in the corner of his tent, wrapped in his comfy robe or fur blanket, trembling in fear. This was the first time he had marched out to battle without God's Presence with him. The confidence the king had up until now was based and founded on the presence of God. His favor. His blessings all come to him through God's Presence. The life he lived up to now was vastly different from the one he was now faced with. His struggles were bigger. His enemies were greater than he. The spirits tormented him, causing him to be at odds with himself. The enemies' armies were more than his. His whole outlook on life has changed, and he didn't know how to deal with it.

My guess was he was doing all he knew to do in his time. Maybe he went on drugs to calm and dull his nerves and anxieties. Maybe he ran to alcohol to numb the pain he felt for disappointing the Lord. Who knows what he experimented with to get the help he needed? Maybe he went to more powerful people than he was to protect himself. He could have even gone to the dark arts, hoping that he could find something to fill the hole in his heart he had created when he disobeyed God. You have to remember - he, too, was human. Yes, a king, but he was human. He had troubles, decisions, worries, and fears just like the rest of us do. So we can only assume he did what his flesh was telling him to do... to survive.

He didn't have the life of Jesus to look to for guidance and support. He could no longer call on Samuel, the Lord's Prophet, to guide him and tell him the correct path to take. He couldn't call on God and scream for help! Christ had not yet died for all our sins, so he hadn't accepted Christ as his Lord and Savior. So he didn't have the protection of the Holy Spirit who lives in us to keep us away from evil spirits like we do. Even if he could converse with God in conversation before this, God had removed Himself from Saul's life. Saul had to have felt that in his mind and body. I know I do when I don't spend as much time with Him as I normally do. My mind tends to see and hear the worst in other people. I get paranoid and worried about things that I wouldn't normally worry about. I get stressed, frustrated, and my temper gets out of control when I don't spend time with God.

Saul had to know that this day at war would be different

than any other time he had faced death. I imagine he was rolled up in a fetal position, lying on the ground of the tent, begging for God to return to his side. Samuel had told him when God removed His Presence from him that God had already found another. So Saul was already paranoid that the new king would come for his throne. But what I don't think he was ready for was a young boy, skinny as a stick, who played the lyre, and who sang soothing songs. I think that when he sent David out to face Goliath, he was already confused and distraught.

When David was trying to reason with Saul that Goliath could be defeated, I believe Saul was afraid for his life. He couldn't think past his fears. So he sent David out to fight Goliath on his behalf. Goliath didn't care who came out. He was an angry, horrible enemy who was there for nothing but war. Have you ever met someone like that? Immovable in their ways? Angry and disgusted by the world they have dealt with? Combative and all they can do is scream and yell obscenities at you? I think as Christians we all have at some point in our walk with God. If you haven't, then maybe your walk with God is a little more lukewarm than you would like to think...

I am not saying that you need to be out marching in the streets, proclaiming the greatness of God. However, you should be out there tearing down some stronghold the devil has placed in your own life. I mean, if you're not overcoming evil in some way or making some changes to become spiritually free, then what was the point of becoming a Christian? You say you're saved, but what are you saved from? What has God done in your life to miraculously change your final destination? Because even though you are covered by the blood of Jesus Christ, you still have to repent of your sins and change your ways. So what changed? How can you read the Bible and not need to change something?

In James 4:17, He says, "*So whoever knows the right things to do and fails to do it, for him it is sin.*"

How can we see someone hungry on the street and not feed them? To see someone lost and not help them find their way? How can we sit by when others are being hurt, lied to, or deceived? By that scripture alone, we are called to act. David saw his king scared of a battle, and he acted. He stepped up and told Saul he would go out and defeat the uncircumcised Philistine who defied God's Law. He prepared himself for battle to the best of his ability, and he went out on the field and faced his giant. He had already overcome so much in his young life. More than most of us who are already older than he was at the time. What more could he lose? He had so much to live for.

His father and brothers may not have put much stock in the anointing, but I believe that David did. I think that when Jesse said he was the one God had chosen and anointed him, David heard loud and clear what God was expecting of his future. God wanted him to be the king over God's People. God wanted him to govern and handle God's Affairs here on Earth. David began walking and talking respectfully to those around him. He carried himself in a way that impressed the king.

You can see this after David defeated Goliath, and King Saul now sees David for who he truly is. King Saul had already met David. He called for him to play the lyre for him, to soothe the spirit that was tormenting him...Hello?!? So why was King Saul asking who he was and who his father was, now after he killed Goliath? Like he had never met him before! His eyes were blind to his selfishness. But now they were wide open and he could see! When King Saul returned to the city and the women were dancing in the streets to praise God and praise the king for his victory, he truly saw David for who he was. Not just in God's Eyes but in the hearts of the people as well. From that moment on, King Saul was aware of his enemy in David.

Even though Saul treated him distastefully, David continued to carry himself with honor and wisdom. Not because he knew he was Saul's replacement to be king, but because I believe that he was now representing God in everything that he did, and he refused to behave in a manner that was dishonorable to God. As Christians, we need to remember that rule. No matter what comes after us or after our family, we have to carry ourselves differently because we now represent God in everything we do. In how we walk, how we dress, how we behave...Everything reflects on our Lord. We need to be Holy, and our character needs to be unblemished. If God sent His Son to die on the cross for our sins and we were saved from the death of that sin, shouldn't we carry ourselves like we are no longer the same? Why do we continue to walk defeated, ashamed, and downcast? Why do we act like we are not worthy to glorify His Name? Your stature should be honorable, dignified, and free. The cost of that freedom was more than we deserved. But you can't keep it to yourself. It was given for others to know and feel as well. So don't live in fear of condemnation.

~ * ~

This leads me to the gifts God gives us who are called to His Side. I feel this is a perfect spot to talk about the giftings God has placed in us to serve our church community and to enable us to reach others who need to know God. Some so many people make a church what God has called it to be. One man or woman, one pastor, does not make a church complete. God tells us that in scripture. He tells us that there are many parts to a whole body. A Head, arms, hands, and feet make up a body, and so there are many different types and kinds of people who make up the church. A pastor can't be at the pulpit and in the nursery at the same time. The gifts that God placed in a janitor are not the same gifts He put in an altar worker. Gifts are not specific, and there are some gifts that each of us carries to serve the church.

We are all called to be Holy. We were called to reflect the Heart of God. Which means we are called to encourage and love one another. We are called to help each other overcome one another's battles. We are called to pray without ceasing and to never give up on one another. We are called to be humbled and meek. Never prideful and boasting of our gifts. We are called to carry the Light that God placed in us for all the world to see. That is a calling that all Christians are asked to achieve for the church body. First things first...

Have you found a church body of believers that you attend regularly? As Christians, God called us to gather together to lift each other higher to get closer to Him. God tells us that iron sharpens iron (Proverbs 27:17), and so gathering together and learning about God makes us better Christians. (Ecclesiastes 10:10) Finding others that we can join our hearts with, to fight the darkness. Joining together gives us the strength to move forward when we are attacked instead of always fighting to breathe. I have spent a large portion of my life feeling like I was being held just under the water's surface, unable to breathe. When I vowed to serve my Lord and Savior, Jesus Christ, I underwent an onslaught of attacks that kept me fighting for my life. Both physical and spiritual.

In 1995, I heard God say, "Write a book. From that moment on, I became intrigued with other writers and began reading books to understand how to do it. At that time, I was in my sophomore year of high school and still hadn't grasped my footing in life yet. Boys entered the scene, and let's just say that I was distracted for a very long time from my calling. Meanwhile, writing was always in the background of my mind, cultivating my voice and strength. God has placed His Gifts in us, and He will provide us with the nutrients and supplies to nourish the seed to grow, but it is up to us to tend to it. To use those gifts and to refine the art of what He has called us to be. So even though God had given me the talent of writing, it was up to me to perfect my skills.

I had to figure out what I wanted to write about. When I first started writing, I was so young that I didn't have access to a computer to type on. Google wasn't even alive yet, and all we really had was AOL email for communication purposes. I didn't even know how to type yet. So in my Junior year of high school, I signed up for a business course as one of my electives and learned how to type on a typewriter. I learned the skills required to type without hunting and pecking for every letter I needed to place in my paragraph. Of course, English classes were mandatory classes to complete high school, so I had access to learn how to learn the basics of writing well. I learned about using different words to convey what I was trying to get my readers to understand. I learned that the story had to be compelling, and it had to draw people's interest as they read it. I learned that there was a proper way to write a sentence, and with the correct punctuation, you could say different things. God gave me my calling, but it was up to me to learn how to do it well.

I went through phases of my life where different parts of

my giftings needed to be perfected. Every person has a combination of giftings in them. We don't just carry one specific gift to glorify God. We carry many. A pastor doesn't just carry the gift of being able to speak well at a pulpit with a microphone. He carries the ability to counsel and lead. Many pastors are gifted in some ways, while others struggle. Some pastors are outgoing and open about their family life. Where others are timid and quiet about the activities of their home life. Some pastors like to pick up trash in the parking lot, and others pay trash men to take the trash out.

So throughout my life, I got distracted by certain parts of my gifts. I would concentrate on areas that I thought God was using me, only to find it to be what I thought was a dead end. However, I discovered the sum of all my experiences has been a recipe for a greater finish for Him. I learned the discipline and hard work of a group could create art when I played in the marching band in high school. I learned discipline when I was a housekeeper for a resort. I learned hard work when I worked in the fast food industry. I learned that there was always more to a person's story when I became a nurse. I learned how consistency and scheduling a marketing strategy could speak to millions when I worked for HoneyBaked Ham.

You see, every stage of my life has brought me to you. Here, in the present, reading this book. God used everything in my life to speak to you about His Heart today. At every stage of my life, God used those experiences to make me a better conveyor of His Word. Everything I have learned and experienced has been a building block to the leader that I am today. Through it all...through the hard, the bad, the hurtful, the painful, the soul-scaring...through it all, every experience has made me into the passionate Christian that I am today. Because with every valley God showed me He was with me.

In every hard lesson, with every soul-crushing blow, I learned something new about God and His love for me. I learned why He made me into the woman I am today. That alone was worth the battle.

However, that was not all I learned. With every strike, I learned how the enemy operated. I learned what his goal was. I obtained knowledge of his tricks. I understood who he was and where he was coming from. If you can learn why your enemy is fighting the way they are, then you can teach yourself how to take down their defenses and learn where he is most vulnerable. It wasn't until I learned about how and why satan fell from God's Grace that I learned that he had no control over me. Once I learned he was just an arrogant, prideful manipulator, he lost all the power over me. I was no longer afraid of him. He became to me an unrepentant child who was only on this Earth throwing a temper tantrum. Granted, he has turned his evil into something unmistakably wicked and destructive. But he has no power over God's Creation. He is beneath us, and he was placed under our feet for eternity. He is angry and frustrated at his losses. It's in our best interest not to join him in his endeavors. The cost of our sacrifice is much greater if we follow him.

So let's get back to who we are called to be. Let me begin by giving you a generic list of people within the church. Of course, there is the Head Pastor. This person or these people are the leaders of the church. Their responsibilities usually entail providing the church body with a message during the times of service. But their duties do not stop there. They are usually an evangelist at heart because they want to see God's Kingdom grow and spread. Now I do want to clarify some differences here. Many feel they need to speak to others about the goodness of God. That is because we are all called to go throughout the Earth to many nations and many tribes to share the good news with everyone we meet. (Mark 16:15) However, not everyone is called to be a pastor. A pastor shoulders many different responsibilities that others do not. Although we are all called to share the good news of the gospel, our titles vary. There are evangelists as well. They travel to many different locations and spread the news of God. Whether in a revival, conference, educational, or meeting format. They are there to help God's People learn and dig deeper into a closer relationship with Him. A pastor ministers to one church community every week. They maintain a relationship with this group of people. They pray, eat, and evangelize within the community together. This pastor often has a stationary building where a large group of people come to participate in the events with their church families. An evangelist often is a guest speaker and travels to speak in front of many people, often never meeting the people they are ministering to.

Some Missionaries go into other parts of the world and preach the gospel to different nationalities. They are also traveling ministers who are usually providing aid, health care, or supplies to the area to show the love of God to those people as they tell them about God. So you see, just because you have a fire burning in you to share the gospel, that doesn't necessarily mean you should go buy a suit and sign up to rent a building or buy a microphone. There are also Young Adult Pastors, Youth Group Pastors, Children's Church Pastors, and Nursery Pastors. Each of these pastors tends to a specific demographic to bring the good news of the gospel to fruition in their lives. Each pastor has the responsibility to tend to their church body's spiritual needs and has dedicated their life to helping them navigate through this life and to join them in seeking God's Will for their constituents' lives.

My biggest recommendation for you to start with is to write down the vision that God has placed on your heart and make a plan to start your journey. Because I have often found that what God has started in you, He will complete, but you will never know what it is that He is doing if you don't begin your walk. Every journey begins with the first step. Most of the time, where you start off thinking that you're going is never where God finally takes you. Again, don't be afraid to take the first step. Always remember that what the enemy can't stop, he will accelerate. This means if you plan on becoming a preacher, satan will do everything in his power to prevent that from happening. He will cause every distraction to disturb your peace about it. He will steal your money, making your resources thin to obtain training or go to college. He will attack your marriage, your children, your workplace, or your family. He will also use those same people to discourage you from your assigned path. My best advice to you is to gather those people who are close to you and tell them what you heard God say that led you to decide to become a pastor. Ask them to join you in prayer and intercession. Ask them to fast on your behalf for the wisdom to walk this path out. That would also include your pastors and leaders from the church that you attend. Just because you feel led to share the Word does not mean you'll get a church right away.

You'll need prayer, time, and patience to walk this calling out. Your pastor is the best person to partner with during this part of your walk with God. He/she has experience in this area that you can learn from while also receiving guidance, prayer, and instruction from someone who knows how to navigate the road that stands before you. You would be naive to think that it would be easy for you to do this without help. I say that not because I don't think you were truly called, but because I know the attacks that are about to unfold upon your life. The moment you declare with your mouth that you want to preach the gospel to the world, the enemy is activated to attack.

In my experiences, I have learned that the enemy only knows what you are up to if you speak out loud into the air. I have searched and tried to find supporting scriptures, to no avail. The only scripture God keeps reminding me of in my spirit man is

Proverbs 17:28: *"Even fools are thought wise if they keep silent, and discerning if they hold their tongue."*

I used to read this and think that God was telling us to talk less, but now, as I try to find scripture to support my belief that satan doesn't know our plans until we speak them out loud into the air, the scripture reads differently to me. I have always believed that it said in scripture somewhere that satan couldn't hear our thoughts or read our minds, and I found comfort in knowing that. Maybe it was a combination of many different scriptures that brought me to this conclusion. However, I still believe it to be true. Why would sharing our testimony be so powerful? (1 Chronicles 16:8) (Revelation 12:11)I believe that when our plan and purposes are set forth into the universe, the agents of darkness— demons then know what we are doing or are set out to do and do everything in their power to not let it happen. They do everything they can to stop, slow down, or change the course of our good plans to further the Kingdom of God. (Ephesians 6:12)

I also believe that the same can be said for the answers God wants us to know and the blessings that He has sent to us. Several times in scripture, the Word tells us that God had answered someone, but something in the spirit realm held them up, and they could not deliver the message to them right away. Read the story of Daniel in this situation in Daniel 10:10. You have to understand there is a war in the spiritual realm that goes on, day and night. Some serve the Lord, and some serve satan. They are constantly in a battle for your soul and for God's Glory.

When I am alone and I am talking with God, I do not need to speak my prayers out loud. When I accepted Christ as my Lord and the Holy Spirit came to live in my heart, my ability to talk and hear directly to the Lord came to me. My soul can speak directly to God all day long with no interruption. My voice doesn't have to be heard to speak to God. However, when I need to command the demons and evil spirits to listen to me, they need to hear my voice. They cannot read my mind. They cannot read my face. No, I have to speak to them with the authority God gave me. If they are tormenting me in my home, I have to tell them they have no authority to be in my home. I have to remind them that I was bought for and paid for by the blood of Jesus Christ. I have to command them to leave me and my house alone. In Jesus' Name.

So when you tell someone else that you want to become a pastor and that you want to share the gospel of Jesus Christ with others around the world, you can be sure an ungodly attack is about to happen in your life. Spiritual, mental, emotional...it can come from anywhere and everywhere. I believe that this will happen regardless of the gift you plan to operate with. This leads me to some of the other areas you might want to serve in the body of Christ. I want to speak to you about another important station in the house of God that is vital to any church, and that is in the Usher Ministry.

I place these ministers' importance right under the pastors because I feel they are vital to any church ministry. A church's ushers are the face of the church. They are the ministry that greets people when they walk in the door. They are the parking ministry that organizes church events. They are the ones who keep the coffee stations friendly and moving forward. They are the ones who hand out communion and keep children safe in the hallways. Ushers are loving, caring, and knowledgeable people who take care of your church members. They also provide support and direction for your Altar Ministry when the pastor asks his church if they need prayers. This ministry is a wonderful ministry to start your journey if you are new to the church and would like to serve and get to know people. Your Head Usher can put you as a greeter, and that is a perfect place where you will get to say hello to everyone who walks in the door! A fantastic, easy way to use your happy heart for the Lord.

Since I just mentioned them, I will dive into the church's Altar Ministry. This ministry is not for the faint of heart. These ministers have gone through years of schooling and training under your church leadership to serve the church members in their walk with God. They do not let just anyone in this ministry because you are guiding and ministering to a person's walk with God. You are a minister sent to the church to help the body of Christ in their darkest and hardest times. You are there to lead and guide these people closer to the Lord. You are there to pray, fast, and speak to areas they are having difficulty in. If you are interested in serving in this position, please go to your pastors and or leaders of the church and ask them to learn more about serving. They can direct you on whether or not this station is right for you. But do not be discouraged if you are told that there is a lengthy process to become an Altar Worker, because more times than not, the process is very strenuous. Most of the time, church membership declarations are needed, background checks are involved, a year to two-year training period, a serving probation time, and mandatory prayer meetings are required for these positions. All are required before you can even begin to serve the church. I have seen many fall short in their endeavors to "work" for the Kingdom of God and "work" at their lives at the same time. Many can't do it. They get burned out because they are trying to do too much. To overcome these needs of both lifestyles is impossible because there is not enough time in the day to do both effectively. This all has to happen while you're working a full-time job, providing for your family, taking care of your children, maintaining your home, caring for your parents, and living your life.

That is why so many people have decided to make their ministry a full-time job. I would love for all of us to be able to work at the church instead of living two separate lives. But I think even if we could do that, the church would be even more ineffective in your community. Unless you can find a way to harmoniously live your life and worship God at the same time. I know, I know. I am being honory again. I think that this is the way God planned for His Church to thrive from the beginning. We have to learn that the change that was made in our hearts when we got saved was not just a quiet, secret no one should ever hear about. When we accept Jesus Christ as our Lord and Savior and we become fully aware of what He did for us, He wants us to tell everyone in our world all about what He is doing. He wants us to tell our best friend all the freedom we feel. He wants you to minister to others, you see, still going through the pains of life. He wants you to share with them how you became free, and that would be harder to do if you were kept away from people inside the walls of a church building all day.

He wants us to continue with our jobs, fully on fire for Him, so that we can share the good news of our deliverance with others that we come into contact with. Most of us, without a job or a reason to get out of the house, won't go anywhere or talk to many people. We are called to change the world, not allow the world to make us afraid to speak His Name. So it is up to us to serve the church and live our lives with Him. Serving the church only becomes difficult if you aren't spending time in His Presence. Because if we are to look like God and to be Christ-like, then what do our hearts and actions look like reflected to God? Are we glorifying Him? When we are serving the church, we become Ambassadors for God. Everything we do reflects on Him. That's why He calls us to be Holy. No matter where or what position we hold in the body of the church.

Another important service in the church is the media and sound ministers. These technology masters serve the church by helping in the sound booth. These ministers are well-trained in their areas to help the church spread the news online and throughout the community. Sound Engineers are the men and women who take care of the soundboard, the speakers, the microphones, and the musical/ praise team's instruments. They also manage the screens that project the words to the songs on the screens, as well as the pastor's message, as needed for the service. This team also manages the equipment that takes care of recording or streaming the service to view online through social media or on website management. So if you are blessed to understand technology, then your place might be to serve the church in this ministry.

Sometimes, as a new believer, you may not have any idea

where you are gifted or where you might fit in, and that's okay. God does not play favorites when it comes to serving him. I often tell those people they can get connected with the church by helping our greeters and ushers. Or better yet, if a ministry interests you and you aren't sure, and you just want to try it out, feel free to offer to aid a minister with their responsibilities on Sunday. There is always room for helpers to clean the church, take the trash out, or help welcome visitors each week. Until you feel like God is guiding you, you will always have a place in your church where you can serve. So don't be afraid to step out and ask your leaders how you can help them. I am sure they will welcome your involvement.

~ * ~

Now I would be neglectful if I didn't address the obvious elephant in the room. Let's be honest. Living in today's day and age, there are many things that we could be afraid of. When God tells us not to live in fear, He doesn't mean to throw caution and common sense away. He's not saying that we should go and put ourselves in danger because there is nothing out there that is dangerous. God has given us wisdom and discernment to keep ourselves safe and healthy. There are things out there that we cannot control. Things like car accidents, train wrecks, airplane crashes, and bank robberies could happen at any time. We cannot control what happens or what other people may or may not do. But what God is saying is to not be consumed with fear. Do not allow it to control your mind, will, or emotions.

There are people in this world who allow the enemy to use them to hurt others. I say it that way because I feel that when we do things to hurt others, we are allowing evil to use us. God gives us free will. So when we choose to do bad things or to say bad things, then we are bad people. However, that is not who God wants us to be. Remember, He wants us to produce good fruits. (Galatians 5:22-23) He wants us to bring joy, peace, patience, love, goodness, kindness, faithfulness, and examples of good self-control out into the world. When we put those gifts out into the lives around us, we are reflecting the goodness of God unto Him.

There have been times in our lives when people have chosen to do really bad stuff to us and that can cause us to be afraid to live our lives to the fullness that God wants for us. So God tells us, that He hates that those people have done those things to you. He says, "Do not worry, child of mine. I will take care of them." (Romans 12:19) (Romans 1:24-27) God doesn't want us to even worry about the vengeance of our tormentors. He doesn't want us to live in a manner that can cause us to be afraid, hurtful, bitter, or angry any longer. God tells us that those emotions are a bondage that keeps us from joy and peace. So we should not entertain those thoughts or worries in our hearts or minds because they will affect everything we do and say.

I know that after the situation with my divorce, it took me a long time to not be affected by what I had just gone through. It has taken time and energy not to feel like I was getting attacked or talked about behind my back. I had to take my fears to God sometimes three to four times an hour to find relief from the torture the enemy was keeping me bound in. Time after time, I was found at the foot of the cross, laying the pain and hurt at Jesus' feet, begging Him to take it from me. Constantly asking God to help me let it go. I had to take control of my thoughts and retrain my brain not to think about the damage that was done.

I literally would start thinking about something bad that

was said or done and I would have to force myself to say something different. Nothing good comes from a custody battle because all that gets done is pain for all parties involved. However, I walked away with the feeling that I was a bad mother for marrying that idiot and having a child with him. That I had done my child wrong by selecting him to be her father. So when those thoughts came to my mind and I began to get upset all over again, I would start saying the truth that God spoke about me. "I am a good mother. I could not control the bad choices he made for his life. I love her with all my heart. I will be here for her when she is ready to come to me." Over and over, I would speak this truth. Sometimes I would speak it out loud so that my ears could hear it said. Over and over, my mind would hear the truth and after some time, the negative thoughts could no longer invade my peace. Don't get me wrong, I still to this day wish I had turned away from him before we got married when God told me not to be with him. However, I took control of my thoughts and the opportunity the enemy had to speak to me on the matter.

Evil does not have the option to be anywhere God's Goodness is. So in your moments of fear, repeat a scripture like Isaiah 41:10, *"Fear not, for I am with you; be not dismayed, for I am your God; I will strengthen you, I will help you, I will uphold you with My Righteous Right Hand."* When we replace the horrible things taking place in our minds with God's Goodness, He comes into the darkness and dispels it. If you are trying to stop listening to bad music with cuss words and talk of killing in it, then listen to good music that glorifies God instead. The only way you will ever break through the torment of darkness in your life is to turn on the Light. With God's Light!

The same can be said of any dark area of your life. Are you

trying to break the habit of smoking cigarettes? Replace the time you would be outside smoking with time reading your Bible instead. Do you want to stop looking at pornography in your life? Then replace that time with watching a Christian movie or reading a good book centered around God. Do you have a problem with a co-worker? Start by telling yourself the good things that she does in the office for the company. There is already too much evil in the world. Let us not add to it by giving it a place in our minds and our hearts. I think as a Christian, wouldn't that defeat the point?

So let God help you overcome the fears in your life, like He did with David's fears. He's not telling you to face the lion and defeat him. He isn't asking you to be king over a people. He is only asking you to overcome your fear and put it back under your feet where it belongs. He only wants you to take your place in this world that He has called you to be. A real estate agent who isn't afraid to make Facebook posts with encouraging scriptures. A hairdresser who listens to praise and worship while cutting hair. A young adult who likes to hang out with their friends play healthy board games, and watch movies that aren't evil. A teen who stands up to a bully who is terrorizing a bus. God wants you to be who you are called to be. But He wants you to be holy and righteous while doing it.

If you are finding that you can't be holy in the job that pays your bills, then you need to find a job where you can be. Or maybe He wants you to change the atmosphere of your workplace. Or maybe He wants you to share the good news of the gospel with your employer. Or maybe He wants to teach you that in Him you have the power to overcome all evil in this world. He wants to discipline your mind to trust Him with all your mind, body, and soul. So that when the time comes for you to stand before your Goliath, you will be as effective as David was. Who knows? Maybe when you become king, you won't make the mistakes David made. Maybe you will have already mastered the art of taking control of your lusts. Maybe you won't be so jealous of another man for having a beautiful wife that you order her to your bed. Maybe you won't try to justify your lusts and have her husband killed.

A man God chose to be king and gave the kingdom to, one day woke up and decided he didn't have enough. He wanted more and he took it. God once said that David was a king after His Heart. God, with all His Knowing Wisdom and power, knew that David was going to sin. He knew that David was going to do something bad, and yet He still chose David to be the king over His People. God knew that David was going to have a child in his sin and that He was going to have to take that baby back to punish David. Yet, God loved him. God knew all of the bad in David's heart, and He still chose that bloodline to bring His Son to life. Do you trust that God can discipline your flesh to be a better king in your life than David was in his?

I believe that you can. Not because I know you. But because I know Him. I know God has brought me through some amazing fears. He brought me through a horrible marriage with an undiagnosed narcissist, divorce, a hurtful custody case, loss of all material belongings, several home break-ins, dead animals on our doorsteps, twelve years of false accusations, three psychological exams, seven heart attacks, two detached eye surgeries, loss of my firstborn child, another difficult early childbirth c-section, and many more since then...Every day I live with the joy of a beautiful daughter who helps remind me that I am a good mother. I am married to a man who reminds me every day that I am lovable and that I am not rejected. I talk to my God, who reminds me that He can discipline my heart and mind to see the good in others and not to be afraid to serve them.

Even now, in my fourth book, He is teaching me that He is ordering my steps in every area of my life. That my faith will not go unrewarded because He is there. My whole life He has trained me to walk in Him and to trust in Him in everything I do and say. He hears my prayers and is faithful to walk with me in my life. That I am not forgotten. I am not doing this alone because HE is with me. If He is for me, then who can be against me? Because HE is everyone everywhere. I do not need to be afraid.

Chapter Four: Discipline

4

I will be honest with you. When I had my vision of David bending over and picking up the five stones that he planned to use that day against Goliath, I was not prepared for God to tell me that discipline was one of the things that David had to overcome. He somewhat caught me off guard because I am currently in a season of learning to discipline myself. After my eye surgery where God healed my heart, I heard him say, "Exercise your Faith." When I pondered the word I heard I heard that day in my walk with God, I considered it both spiritually and physically. My heart had not been able to pump blood correctly to my body for over three years. So now I found my doctor telling me I had to build my muscles back up to be strong enough to do the things I used to be able to do before the heart troubles.

However, spiritually, I had to exercise and begin to walk my faith out with fear and trembling. Up until now, I have published three books and I have not paid for any advertising or marketing of those books in any way. I have not scheduled any book tour signings or scheduled conferences to speak as God showed me to do. I had only self-published them and placed them on Amazon to start selling them there. However, I knew my plans would need to build and grow before I could schedule to do book signing tours and appearances. When I finished the first book, He showed me a vision of where I was going to become that person now. He wanted me to teach others to walk in the same freedoms that He had walked me through. After I had that vision, it almost paralyzed me. But I took a deep breath and found peace; solace that it was not time to walk it out yet. That I had things He wanted me to do before that would come to pass. I knew I had to write several books and get them online, pay for a year of promotions, and then start making announcements to start the signing tours. I wasn't anywhere close to getting that stuff done yet. So I was safe.

I wrote Out of the Ashes, The Fallen Ones. I wrote Out of the Ashes, The Choice. I began writing Out of the Ashes, The Flame, and after the first several chapters of that book, God stopped me from writing that to write this one. Stepping Stones. Halfway through writing this book, God gave me the task of writing a program to publish books for churches to use to train their altar ministers to adequately help the church heal from the attacks of the darkness. You see, no matter how quiet His Voice is, He is always speaking. Always and over time, you can discipline your heart and mind to hear Him in everything. You can train your body to overcome physical limitations, and your brain and ears are muscles too. So they can be trained to build up their strength to do what God is calling them to do. Exercise your Faith.

That was exactly where young David found himself right after Jesse anointed him with the horn or anointing oil. David needed to exercise his faith and strength in God a little more. He needed to practice what God had already given to him. He had to teach himself to use the slingshot that God had brought to him. So God sent the lion to attack his sheep. God needed him to practice his slingshot skills. David more than likely used his slingshot to practice his aim on the lion that day. He probably missed the lion. Scriptures do not tell us this, but I feel that David was human. Just like us. He had to practice using the slingshot to be able to use it confidently before he could go into battle with it. David had to train. Just like we would have. The Bible does tell us that he had to physically take on the lion to overcome the animal. Still strengthening his body and muscles. But God wastes nothing in His Lessons to overcome something. Who knows, maybe David wanted to kill the lion with the slingshot but failed. Maybe David hadn't followed God's Voice as closely as he should have. He still needed more practice. There was still more he needed to learn.

So later, God sent the bear. David might have tried again with his slingshot, but he used a different type of rock this time. He might have learned after the lion that he had to swing his slingshot harder to gain the speed he needed to eject the rock. He might have needed a different tilt of his arm to force the rock to go further so that the animal didn't get so close to him. Maybe David needed to act quicker when God told him to release the rock. He needed more practice. There is always more to learn.

So, who knows, when he fired at the bear, he might have been able to hit him, but this time the aim wasn't right. He may have aimed for his head but hit the side of the bear instead. He missed again. But he still had to physically kill the bear. Building the strength of his body. That day, after his failed attempts with the bear, who knows, maybe David set out to hone his skills with his slingshot and spent more time in the field with God getting it right. He needed to spend time with God to understand His Guidance. He needed time with God to clearly understand God's Direction. He needed time to teach himself how to effectively use his slingshot. David may not have known why he was so obsessed with perfecting the art of the slingshot yet, but he knew it would be vital in God's Plans for his life.

You see, we may not know why we are going through the hardships that we are going through, but God wastes nothing in His Lessons. Maybe He is trying to teach us to be more patient when we drive in the city. Maybe He is trying to teach you that there is a more effective way to speak to your co-workers to get a better response from them. Maybe God needs you to spend more time with Him so that He can discipline you to hear His Voice clearly instead of the other stuff around you. That way, He doesn't have to yell at you next time He needs to get your attention. Maybe, just maybe, God is teaching you the discipline you need to have for the next part of your journey. God wastes nothing in His Lessons.

When my second daughter was born, the geneticist who came to talk to us told us the difficulties she would have as she got older. He told us that children with Down Syndrome had varying difficulties in learning comprehension. He explained to us that we may have to repeat how to do something many times to get her to fully understand why and how to do something. When she started to get older and started to crawl and do things for herself, I truly understood the concept of having patience. I often wonder if God looks down at some of us like I do with my daughter. If He gets frustrated and upset because we just can't get why He keeps telling us to do these things a certain way, and we clearly don't listen to Him. I wonder if He sits back exhausted when we go to bed and if He says to Himself, "Well, we will try that again tomorrow."

Or if it upsets Him when we go away mad and angry because we don't understand why we can't have things our way. When He is just trying to show us that going that way or doing it that way will get us hurt. If it hurts Him to let go of us, to teach us the lesson the hard way. If He cries in private because He hates to discipline us, but He knows that it's for our good. I am sure that it hurts His Heart as our Heavenly Father. He made us. He created us in our mother's womb. He carried us when we were broken. He loved us when we were abandoned. He laughed with us when we were silly. He cried with us when we were sad. He's been with us through every moment. Protecting us when we needed it. Keeping us from getting hurt when others put us in danger. He has been there through it all when we were younger. Why would He not be here now? Now that we know He is there to help us understand life. When we need to hone our skills and discipline ourselves to grow into the person He has called us to be. Of course, He is. He tells us He collects our every tear! (Psalms 56:8)

So, how does God want us to be disciplined? How does following Him teach us about being better? I like the English Standard Version translation of the Word found in Hebrews 12:11. It tells us everything we need to know about why God wants us to be disciplined in His Ways.

"For the moment all discipline seems painful rather than pleasant, but later it yields the peaceful fruit of righteousness to those who have been trained by it."

Peaceful fruit of righteousness. Wouldn't that be nice? To be able to walk through this life peacefully and be righteous?

Not to have to argue with others about our beliefs. To not have fear, anger, jealousy, hate? So maybe there is something to His Plans for our discipline, huh? What do you think? So what else does God say about discipline? In 1 Corinthians 9:27, He says,

"But I discipline my body and keep it under control, lest after preaching to others I should be disqualified."

So we must control ourselves so that when we tell others about the goodness of God, they will believe us. They will know we are telling the truth and they will see a different person than the one they used to know. Or maybe they will see something good in us that they also want. Okay, okay. We hear you, God. So, what does God say about how to control our bodies?

"If anyone thinks he is religious and does not bridle his tongue but deceives his heart, this person's religion is worthless." James 1:26

"Draw near to God, and He will draw near to you. Cleanse your hands, you sinners, and purify your hearts, you double-minded." James 4:8

"Finally, brothers, whatever is true, whatever is honorable, whatever is just, whatever is pure, whatever is lovely, whatever is commendable, if there is any excellence, if there is anything worthy of praise, think about these things. What you have learned and received and heard and seen in me—practice these things, and the God of peace will be with you." Philippians 4:8-9

"We destroy arguments and every lofty opinion raised against the

knowledge of God, and take every thought captive to obey Christ," 2 Corinthians 10:5

"He drew me up from the pit of destruction, out of the miry bog, and set my feet upon a rock, making my steps secure." Psalm 40:2

There are many more scriptures in the Bible that teach us how God wants us to discipline and control our body parts. I will leave that to you to look into on your own time. However, I want to spend some time talking to you about the intentions of your heart. God tells us that from our hearts flows everything in our life. So if that's the case, wouldn't we need to take a closer look at what is in our hearts? If we go back to scripture, the Bible tells us that as David was running his mouth off in Saul's camp about the audacity of the uncircumcised Philistine, he was told that the person who fought Goliath would have the king's daughter's hand in marriage, he would be rich, and his family would be clear of all their debts. Which some would say. "We'll there is David's motivation." But David didn't start talking trash about winning the battle for her. He didn't start professing his strength to become rich and to make his father proud of him and wealthy.

He just went on about his way through the camp with the attitude that he couldn't believe this uncircumcised Philistine. Who does he think he is? To come against God in such a disgraceful way. You see, you have to remember, that in this age of time, the fear of God was made evident. In their perspective timeline, their lineage knew about God removing Sodom and Gomorrah, Joseph was cast into slavery, Moses spoke to Egypt's Pharaoh to release God's People, and a Woman of God (Deborah) served as Judge (Prophet). All of this happened a little less than a thousand years before Saul became king. That's like our elders remembering World War 1 or when Henry Ford started the first eight-hour-a-day, five-day work week establishing the standard for all companies across the U. S. (Ugh! Gag!)

The lessons of the things they have learned may have felt like ages but they were still fresh in their lives. Just like many of our grandparents remember women not being allowed to vote or black people remember being slaves. The history was long ago but still hurts. People in King Saul's time lived and operated in the knowledge and understanding that God was alive and they better listen. Unlike our elders today who think God is not real and he was just a myth made up to scare people into behaving. I am reminded of the importance of knowing our history as write this because I had to look up on the internet what happened back in 1925. Thank God for the internet! Because we would never be able to mark such important dates for learning purposes. I feel that if we don't memorialize or journal life and its lessons then our minds and hearts will easily forget.

As soon as you can, start a journal of all the things God has taught you each day. Because one day, your children or your grandchildren will ask you to tell them about the goodness of God in your lifetime. You want to be able to recall all the details of the times He has met you where you were to help you. You want to be able to recall your exact thoughts and feelings of fretting when you needed money, but then God came along and reminded you that HE always provided for you. Your children will ask you why you prayed for them for so long. Your grandchildren will ask you who Jesus is and why you worship Him and go to church. They will want to hear more about who you used to be before you were old and brittle and you will want to be able to tell them. You want to be able to tell them in your own voice and with your own words, not someone else's. Even if you pass away before Jesus returns, your loved ones will want to know more about your journey with God. Make sure your legacy isn't left to those who thought they knew you. Leave behind a greater part of your history.

So when we read about David's righteous walk through camp that day, he tells us exactly what his motivations were that led to his victory on that battlefield. He was fighting to honor God. He was upset that no one would rise up and defend God. He was passionate about who God was. Why weren't the king's men? I believe the fear of the king had spread throughout the camp. For forty days and nights Goliath had tormented and spit on God. He threatened God's Men and trash-talked the respect, honor, and fear that had built God's People. Why wouldn't anyone stand up to the Philistines? I think David felt God's Anger. I think He had spent enough time with God to know God's Heart. He didn't have to ask God what he needed to do. He immediately felt God call him to the front of the army.

David's heart was forged with God's Heart because he knew Him. He had spent time with God. In David's low, poor, uneventful shepherd life he had time to seek after God and when you spend so much time understanding why God is keeping you where He placed you, you begin to understand more about who HE is. You understand why He thinks and feels the way that He feels. It is only when you pull away from Him that you begin to lose sight of Him. That's when we make mistakes and sin. We take our minds off the finish line and fall into the path of the racer beside us.

Have you ever seen a NASCAR race or a track meet where the car in the lead veers to the left just a little and it sends them spiraling out of control in the paths of the cars next to him? If you start looking to the left, your hand pulls your steering wheel to the left. You start looking to the right and you pull your steering wheel to the right...And before you know it you lost the race and wrecked a million-dollar car! This is what I feel David did after his battle with Saul was won and he was put on the throne. He was rich and powerful. He was a great king to God's People but He took his eyes off of seeking God when he got what he wanted and looked down. He then saw Bathsheba bathing in her tub on the roof of her husband's house and here entered sin.

His heart and mind needed to keep seeking after God's Heart and Face to remain pure and holy. There would never have been a mark against him if he had stayed on the path that God had called Him to. Who knows?!? God might have had his perfect wife already picked out if David had waited for her. However, I feel that in David's sin, he activated his curse throughout his bloodline from that moment on. We see David's children fall from God's Glory in more destructive ways than those of the kings before them.

If you think about it, Jesus could have been born in a castle adored by thousands. Not only the Son of God but the Son of a King of David if he would have stayed in his lane. If he would have stayed in God's Disciplines and within God's Lessons. What could we say about how pure our walk would be if our ancestors had learned from their ancestor's walk? If they would have remained pure and holy? Let's go deeper. How good could your children's lives be with God if they knew the battles you had overcome through God's Disciplines? What if you could train yourself to follow after God and be who God has called you to be?

What if you stopped seeking after drugs and alcohol to go after God and His Kingdom? What if you stopped spending money at the bar and the race track to seek God first? What if you dedicated your life's purpose to being who God has called you to be instead of who your friends think you are? I believe you could change the trajectory of your whole family's bloodline! I believe you could on to college and find the woman or man God has created for you. I believe you will overcome so many obstacles your family could write books after your legacies.

You see, not because you are great but because God is. God is a Way Maker. You can't do all the things in this life that God has called for you to do without God being by your side in it. Well, you could, but I would have to ask, how did that work out for you? So how do we change our hearts? How do we learn to trust again? How do we turn hatred into love, grace, and mercy. God tells us we can't trust our flesh and we learned what God says in scripture about how to control our bodies. So why can't our minds be controlled the same way? Yes, we need to go back to scripture and find out exactly what God says about controlling our minds.

"Set your minds on things that are above, not on things that are on earth." Colossians 3:2

"Therefore, preparing your minds for action, and being sober-minded, set your hope fully on the grace that will be brought to you at the revelation of Jesus Christ." 1 Peter 1:13

"Finally, brothers, whatever is true, whatever is honorable, whatever is just, whatever is pure, whatever is lovely, whatever is commendable, if there is any excellence, if there is anything worthy of praise, think about these things. What you have learned and received and heard and seen in me—practice these things, and the God of peace will be with you." Philippians 4:8-9

* * *

"Do you not know that if you present yourselves to anyone as obedient slaves, you are slaves of the one whom you obey, either of sin, which leads to death, or of obedience, which leads to righteousness?" Romans 6:16

That last verse there in Romans 6:16 says all we need to know. We are a slave to something— We can be a slave and obey the darkness that leads to death or we can follow Christ which leads to life! I believe David knew that the day he was walking around the camp that day, appalled that someone out there wanted to defy the Lord God and knowingly live in darkness. However, as I say that and my mind begins to wonder why the Philistine people were so upset and defiant to God's Love. That's why our lineage and history are so important to who we are today. If you research the people of Philistine and Gath, they were comprised of people who were from one of Noah's sons.

He had three sons and their wives on the Ark that God told Noah to build before the days when God flooded the whole Earth. Their names were Shem, Ham, and Japheth. Several different sources that I found said the Philistine people came from Ham's line. If you remember, Ham became angry and upset with Noah after the flood. He found Noah, drunk and passed out in his tent. From what I could find out about the Philistine people through history and archaeological digs, these people thought they were better than other tribes. They sought after money and worldly possessions over fame and power.

So when Ham found his father drunk and passed out like that, he thought badly of his father and turned around and sang a curse incantation over Noah. It was said that the evil curse he sang over him rendered Noah sterile and unable to have any more children. There was much speculation online on websites like TheTorah.com that spoke of the evil thing Ham did was more than just seeing his father, Noah naked. They speak several different questions that several other times in history when a father had sexual relations with a daughter or if a mother had relations with a son there was an Incest Curse God would place on the bloodline. This made sense to me because all of Noah's forefathers had many children. Noah only had three sons. But in this part of the story, Ham did something to his father that was so evil that Noah turned around and cursed him for doing it. He says that Canaan would be a slave to his brothers. I found it to be interesting how history played out because Shem's line produced the heirs to Abraham, Judah, Jesse, and King David. Which led to the birth of Jesus Christ.

So as you can see when we discipline our bodies and our minds we can drastically affect our children, grandchildren, and great-grandchildren's lives. At any point in history, an undisciplined, unsaved family member has brought some sort of hardship over us. So it is important that we discipline ourselves to overcome the evil in our world, so we train our children how to do so as well. Because we all know the hurt and pain that our parents left us with and we don't want to pass it down to our children. Someone needs to break the cycle. It needs to stop with you.

Discipline is a noun and a verb. Its first definition is, "The practice of training people to obey rules or a code of behavior, using punishment to correct disobedience." When I first read that, I got a little defensive. Because I immediately heard the part about being punished. As an adult, I don't typically think that adults need to be punished. That is normally a practice I think about with children and then the Holy Spirit checked me. Have you ever felt the Holy Spirit nudge you in the gut and say, "Come again? You want to stop and think about what you're doing or saying here before you get into trouble?" After the gut check, I can always see the Holy Spirit's Face looking at me with his head cocked to the side and his hands on his hips like my mother when she used to tell me to stop and think long and hard before I took another step. After that first reading of the definition, I felt that check.

So I went back to the definition and read a little more. The second definition said this, "A branch of knowledge, typically one studied in higher education." As I read that definition I understood where God was coming from. We have to discipline ourselves to go deeper into our relationship with the Lord. God says to us in *Hebrews 5:13-14 KJV, "Anyone who lives on milk, being still an infant, is not acquainted with the teaching about righteousness. But solid food is for the mature, who by constant use have trained themselves to distinguish good from evil."* We start off eating a bottle. We understand that Jesus Christ died on the cross to save us from our sins. Woohoo! We are saved. But as we dig deeper we read and understand that He was beaten and made to carry His Cross to the hillside where they took His clothes and made Him all but naked. Then ran large steel spikes and drove them into His Hands and Feet. They nailed Him to the cross where they mocked, tormented, and tortured Him. Instead of water to drink, they gave Him soured vinegar on a sponge. They put a crown of thorns on His Head and mocked Him because His followers said He was King of the Jews. They pulled His whiskers from His beard from His Face. They stabbed through His ribcage with a steel-tipped spear to be sure He was dead. Before allowing His Mother and friend to take His Body to be prepared for burial.

You see we know that He died. As a child we know He

suffered for us and some children can understand He died. But today on Easter Sunday my mother was teaching the young children in her children's class about the events that happened and one boy's broken heart stood out to her. So she told me about it. I know this young boy, so I know he has heard the story before but he apparently didn't understand it. As she was telling him that Jesus died on the cross, he got upset. He couldn't believe Jesus had died. He kept questioning her in disbelief. "He's dead?" She explained to him that if he calmed down she would tell him the rest of the story. Of course, we know that He rose to life again and ascended to Heaven to be with God. To sit at His Right Hand and intercede for us. But as a child, we don't truly understand what happened that day.

As I was reading about what was done to Jesus that day to write about it to you, as you read I told you that they gave Jesus vinegar to drink instead of water on the sponge. But then my husband comes in with a Facebook reel about Roman history in disgust and tells me about how people used to go to the bathroom and back then they didn't have toilet paper to wipe. They had a stick with a sponge on the end for people to use to wipe and after one person would use the bathroom they would wipe with that stick and throw the sponge and stick in the bucket on the side that had vinegar in it to disinfect the sponge for the next person. The reel said nothing about Jesus. It was a post about history and how far we had come. However, we felt the Holy Spirit's nudge that there was more to it. People are evil. People are horrible. People are nasty, ugly, vile creatures. I'll leave that there. But as an adult, we understand what Jesus did for us.

As we discipline our hearts, we have to train ourselves to understand the depths of God's Love for us. We understand in His Word why He tells us to do the things that He asks of us. We learn why He has brought such punishment down upon our people. As an adult we no longer drink milk from a bottle, we understand the meat of who God is and in His Righteousness, we can learn how to share the truth with others. So that they can move away from the bottle also. They can teach their children and their friends the truths of the goodness of God that leads us all to repentance. So they can understand the truths that we read in scripture. Not so we can just read it, but we can understand the motives of God's Heart. So we can lovingly correct our brother or sister at church in a Godly way that they are walking down the wrong path.

You see as a child and as a new Christian, we would see them sinning and we would be like a loud tattletale on the playground. We would start yelling for an adult to come and fix the problem. We would scream for someone else to come handle the kid who was doing something bad. But as an adult, we can go over to the brother who is sinning and take him to the side and teach him about how God wants him to act. We show him in scripture that there is a reason why God tells us to not give into those sins. We pray with him and lead him to God to repent. God wants us to grow up and to get away from our childish ways. We need to find the way that is acceptable to Him. God tells us that if we can't operate in love, then our religion is worthless as a clanging cymbal. If you can't help others be better, then we are without purpose. He can't use us in the church. Or better yet how could He trust us out in the world to lead others to Him?

We sit in church and I have heard so many get upset that the pastor hasn't chosen them to preach or to do something in the church. I have known people who have tried to pay off the pastor to give them the microphone. I have seen belittling, degrading, gossiping, lying, and backstabbing happen in the church. I have witnessed a wife speaking so horribly about her husband for so long that he finally fell in love with another woman at work because she treated him like an equal. I have seen men in the church act so inappropriately to their wives in front of others, she left him and the church because she was mortified by his actions and speech. I have seen leagues of teens leave the church because they couldn't understand who they were to God, now that they graduated from high school.

I know the church is made up of people. Living, breathing, busy people. But as Christians aren't we supposed to be better than this? Should we as a church family be able to prevent this kind of thing from happening? Discipline starts in the home. Promise Keepers and Baptist Press did a study and gathered some pretty amazing statistics about the effectiveness of someone being saved in the home and if they go to church. I quote them here:

"Another survey found that if a child is the first person in a household to become a Christian, there is a 3.5% probability everyone else in the household will follow. If the mother is the first to become a Christian, there is a 17% probability everyone else in the household will follow. However, when the father is first, there is a 93% probability everyone else in the household will follow."

93% of families in the United States of America will see their whole family saved and move onto a relationship with God after they graduate if the FATHER leads them! Fathers you need to wake up and get involved in your church! Your children's future depends on it. Fathers, you are the head of the household. Yeah, women, I said what I said. I have also heard it said, "Yeah my husband is the head of the home but the wife is the neck and she tells the head which way to go!" That, my friends, is evil and from a spirit straight from hell. It is called the Jezebel Spirit. If you want to read about the woman who carried this evil in the flesh you can find her story in 1 Kings 18. If you speak that statement, stop immediately. That is not the relationship God calls for there to be in your marriage. That is not the woman God wants you to be. Don't be her!

I know most ministers will point out that if you want to be the perfect Godly woman then go to Proverbs 31 and yes, all scripture is great. But every woman is different. We don't all like to get up before everyone else in the house and we don't always like to be the last to go to sleep. Not every woman can cook and sew linens. Not every woman was made to buy property and not every girl wants a man who is known at the gates of their community. But do you want to know what every woman is made for? They are made to serve and worship God with all their heart. Whether they are a teacher or a dispatcher for the police department. A stay-at-home mother or a woman who can't have children. Regardless of the life that you have had up until now,
I am telling you that God made you to worship Him. He loves you and sent His Son to die on the cross so that He can have a relationship with you.

There are many honorable women of God in the scriptures that you can read about. There is Deborah, the prophet/judge. There is Queen Esther or Ruth. There are so many women that we can learn from in the Bible. By all means, read about them all, and let God speak to you about who He created you to be! I am sure there is a magnificent testimony welling up inside you. Make sure you share it with me sometime! But I believe with my whole heart that God made us all different for a reason. So that we could go out to our friends, to our communities, to our children's schools and tell them about the word of God. To tell them how wonderful HE is and what HE has done for us. So that we can share it with everyone everywhere. That goes for men, women, and children! We are all called to overcome our mountains and to serve and share the gospel with others.

I feel that we all could do a better job of learning to discipline our minds and bodies unto God. In other words, we need to learn to submit ourselves fully to Him to be able to be used by Him. We have to overcome self-doubt, obedience, and fear before we can all grow and learn to submit to Him. Through the lens of submission, we can understand where God is taking us. Because if He can't trust us with the little things to overcome then how can He trust us with the more difficult things we will face as we move forward? When I say move forward, I mean when He can finally start giving us meat to eat and to start raising others to trust in Him. Because isn't that His Goal? To get us to a point where He doesn't have to hold our hand so tightly when walking across the street?

Like a parent, at first, He had to be with us every second of the day because we couldn't be trusted not to pull stuff off the table or pull the trash can down on ourselves. Like a parent, He wants to get us to a place where He can give us a mission and HE can know with all His Heart that we will do exactly as HE said to do and complete it for HIS GLORY. Not our own. So that when He tells us to go and speak to the church about the lessons HE has taught us, we will deliver it with honor and respect due to the mantle HE has placed on us. God wants to give us more responsibilities and to further our careers in ministry but can He do it safely knowing we will not steal glory from Him? Or know that we won't slip back into our old habits of lying, speaking foul language, or cheating on our wives?

At some point in time, every Christian has to grow up and take responsibility for their walk with God. The good and the bad must be recognized and dealt with before He can trust that we will stay the course that He has given to us to bring Him Glory. That means we have to be disciplined to behave in a way that brings Him Honor and Glory. Because if you remember He told us that if we can't control ourselves then our religion is worthless to those who are watching us. You see every non-believer is looking at everything we do to tear us down. They want us to make mistakes and act like them, because if we act like them then we are in turn liars like them.

I am torn about today's headlines, because there is always news about Trump doing something wrong or saying something wrong. He claims to be a Christian but the world says that a Christian shouldn't act like him. That if he was as he says he is then he would be held to a greater standard because of the great mantle that has now been placed on his life. As President of the United States of America, any president has the responsibility to carry themselves with dignity, honor, and respect of an office like his. But as a Christian President, he bears the name of God himself. The Bible tells us that He places people in these positions and that if He placed them there then we are to respect and honor their position. Now, don't get me wrong, like I said I am torn because I feel a lot of the scrutiny that Trump is getting is unwarranted. With today's false media and TV reports, I feel they're more propaganda ambulance chasers than actually reporting the truth, but isn't that how satan prefers it?

He takes part of the truth and twists it to make you hear or see something that is not real. Look at what he did to Eve in the Garden with the apple. Look at what he did to Job.

Look at what he tried to do to manipulate Christ in the wilderness. He is constantly trying our patience, to tempt us away from the hand of God. So discipline yourselves to speak against him or leave the areas where you are being tempted. God tells us that if you resist the devil he will flee from you. (James 4:7) But I feel that in my walk, he flees a lot faster when I tell him to leave me alone in Jesus; Mighty Name. Almost like I am kicking his tail down the road, away from me while he's running. I say it out loud so that he and all his minions can hear me profess the name of Jesus Christ, my Lord to them. Just so we are all on the same page.

It takes a great measure of discipline to not be afraid of the things we can't see and the things we can't control. That's where and when we build our faith. When I was young I was like the little kid at the beginning of the Pixar/Disney movie Monsters Inc. I could've sworn there was a monster's hand over the chair by the closet. Only to feel ridiculous to realize that it was only a shirt hanging out of the closet. I would close my eyes and go back to sleep only to be awakened by something I heard. I won't go into detail because I will not give attention to evil that way but it was then I was made aware of the reality of the things in the night. I ran to my parent's room and was dismissed with the "Go back to bed. It was only a dream," speech. But I knew right then that night that it was not.

I went to my Bible and began to understand what I was dealing with. We didn't have a TV or radio for entertainment. My father had gotten rid of them because they were stealing our time and our minds...That's a different story. But at that time I was kind of glad those electronics weren't there because God had me on a different path. He taught me things that stuck with me all through high school and guided me into adulthood. There is evil in this world and it will stop at nothing to distract, remove, distort, manipulate, and take away the will that God has placed over our lives. The darkness is there and now it has an endless source of ways to reach children like never before in history.

The screen time addiction in the world is real. Oh, you disagree with me? Try to tell your children they can't have their tablets or phones for a whole week and see how they react. If your child is like mine, then there is a problem. She became rude, hateful, and even indignant about her tablet. If you were talking and she couldn't hear her tablet she began screaming and hitting us. We couldn't get her to listen when asked to do things. She became such a problem for me to get ready to go to school one day and I had had enough of the fighting with her. I took it out of her hands and she became so angry with me, that she picked up a table chair from the kitchen table and threw it at the window.

She was a weak, little six-year-old girl at the time and she picked up a heavy, wooden kitchen chair and threw it. I took it away that day. I kept it away for six months. This tablet just had a few episodes of Sesame Street on it and a couple of learning games to help her learn letters, numbers, and colors. It was not hooked up to the internet. She didn't have access to TV shows, YouTube, or the internet. But folks the addiction was real. The next few days after I took it away, she went on a house-wide hunt for the thing. Turning over every rock, cushion, and door she could get her hands on. Of course, I had to lock it away for the time to keep it from her, but it was a rough couple of weeks for me.

After the reality settled in that she wasn't getting it back for the foreseeable future she started to adjust. She started playing with her toys and reading her books again. Her attitude problem and difficulty issues started to fade. She started to participate in family events and started to play with us again. We had given the tablet to her as a gift for Christmas and at first, she wasn't that interested in it. But I started to teach her how to do things on it for herself and her interest in it started to grow. I won't lie; she is a very active child who always needs attention. She also is an only child and as I have told you before she was born with Down's Syndrome. So her neediness is relentless.

She constantly looks to me as her guide to know how she should feel about things. If her daddy and I burst into laughter about something that happened on a TV show we are watching, we have to immediately rush to her aid because she starts freaking out and crying. She would only react that way because she was scared and she didn't know what just happened. So she taught herself to look to me to explain things before reacting, which has helped immensely...unless you're me. It's exhausting. She never disconnects. She never goes off and plays quietly in her room. She never sits quietly and watches a movie. She is full throttle, full of energy until it's bedtime, always on the go kind of girl. She's exhausting.

So when we got her the tablet all that changed. She calmed down and began to focus and concentrate on the lessons. She began to learn how to operate it and find things on the device for herself and slowly she started to need me less. At least for a little while. Which gave me a few moments to breathe. The tablet also gave us the ability to go out into public and enjoy friends and family again. Since the day she was born, she hated going inside busy restaurants. After a while, she was diagnosed with Social Anxiety Disorder. This was common for children with Down's because they can't read social cues like you and I. Of course, three years of isolation due to Covid didn't help her at all. Before Covid she was outgoing and would go into church and would wave at the other church members she knew and smile. But when COVID scared everyone, her whole life did too. Normally the inability to read cues makes the child with Down's too friendly. They don't understand that they can't touch you or brush your hair because it's not the right time. They don't understand that everyone's laughter isn't at them. They can't understand why someone is crying. They can't understand the difference between laughing at someone or laughing with someone. They will never be able to understand these things without a lot of help and time.

So if we would go out to eat with family she knew, she couldn't get over the fact that there were a lot of people there that she did not know and she was very uncomfortable. Where most Down Syndrome children are outgoing and talk a lot, my baby is withdrawn and observant. Where most children love hugs and love to show affection, my baby needs personal space like the kind you give a porcupine. She hates being touched and dislikes you looking at her even more. So it has taken a lot of time and limitless trying and get her to understand that it was okay. We were with her and we wouldn't let anyone hurt her. However, it wasn't until the tablet came into play that her social anxiety disappeared. She was able to focus on that instead of the stuff that was happening around her.

That was enough to make outings okay again. Then after a while, it got easier and now you have to have the tablet and a basket of french fries waiting for her or the crying and screaming break loose. She is always a work in progress. But you see where her addiction came from, right? She NEEDED that thing to feel like she could handle all of the stuff around her. She HAD to have it or her life was out of her control. She COULD NOT go out in the world without it.

Sound familiar? I know. It's okay. All addiction that the enemy throws on us is led by the same evil spirits. The same darkness that came on my baby girl is the same darkness that you fight every day. But do you know something? You can break the hold the darkness of that addiction has over your life. You can discipline your mind and body to let go of that item, person, or chemical. When I first realized that morning that my girl had a problem, yes I took the tablet away. Out of sight, out of mind. Right? No, that's a lie straight from hell and you and I both know it. The moment you tell your body that it can't have those things anymore, it starts screaming and yelling at you. If you could see your spirit man and your physical man as two different separate individuals you would see the reaction the addiction has on you. You stop giving the body the thing that you are addicted to and the inner spirit man starts to pick up the chair to throw it through the window.

Your mind, body, and spirit are out of alignment with God. That's what the addiction has done to you. It has taken God off His Throne in your life and replaced Him with alcohol, drugs, or a person. Whatever you're addicted to, it has taken over your life. That's why we need God's Help to break the tie it has on you off of you. When I first took her tablet away, I knew that was not going to be it. When she came home and couldn't find it, she began to panic. Her panic came from the lies the enemy was speaking to her ears and she was listening to it. If you don't have your tablet, then you won't be able to have fun again. If you don't have your tablet your family won't want to go out in public with you again. If you don't have your tablet, then you won't be able to learn the things you need to learn without it. My daughter is non-communicating so I made those lies up because I do not know what she was hearing. But I do know how the darkness works. I want you to know that there is evil in the world and this is how it is using you, hurting you, and keeping you from real joy.

Those lies continued for a couple of days before I knew God and I needed to intervene for her. She spent several days in that search and find it mode. Her obsessive, repetitive nature was controlling her something fierce. So I started to talk to her and tell her what God's Truths were for her. I started to pray with her and talk to God with and for her. I held her when she cried in frustration. I prayed over her while she slept. I gave her other things to do instead of watching that tablet. I taught her to spend her time wisely. To clean up and put toys away. I spoke to her and told her not to listen to that liar who was telling her hurtful things in her head. That she was a bright, smart little girl and that she could do all things. I told her she was strong and mighty to overcome this.

I began to use the truth in God's Word to break the yoke that bondage had on her. With every good word spoken over her, her attitude changed. With every, "Good job, Baby Girl!" she regained the confidence she lost. With every prayer, she reclaimed her joy to do all the other things in the house that she loved doing. Like building forts and playing with her stuffed animals. After about six months we were able to reintroduce the tablet in small increments on a reward basis. It became the tool that was used to overcome her problems with not listening when she was told to do something. However, never long enough to regain it's control it had on her.

You see, I think you and God can overcome the same problems with your addictions. You can discipline your mind, body, and soul to submit to God and release the bondage of slavery, sin, and death that it has placed on you. First things first. You have to stop and get rid of the things you are addicted to. If you are addicted to porn, delete it or throw it in the trash. If you are addicted to alcohol, pour it down the drain. If you are addicted to drugs, then flush it down the toilet. If you are addicted to a person, then stay away from them or keep them away from you. Regardless of what you're addicted to, you have to get away from it right now. Just like I did with Sammie's tablet. Get it away from your mind and body.

The next step is you have to train your mind. You have to control your mind away from the lies the darkness has taught you. First master the art of shutting his lies down. When he speaks a lie to you, you refute it. Then say something truthful that God speaks and says over you. For example...The darkness tells you as you are walking down the street, "You see those people over there outside having drinks and having a good time? You'll never be able to do that again, because you no longer drink. Your friends won't want to hang out with you anymore."

That's your cue to refute the lie. "That is a lie that is straight from hell and you know it. If they are my friends they will do other things with me that are fun. We can play baseball in the community league or we can hang out at the movies. The world doesn't revolve around alcohol. God says that a good friend is closer than a brother! They will still be there." You see, the enemy's only goal here is to keep you out of the game. He wants you to be sat in the penalty box; unable to serve and out of commission. Because who knows?!? Maybe if you were sober you would realize that your friends look up to you. The darkness knows that if he can keep you away from God then he can keep your friends in bondage also. Because if you are free, you will free them as well. Freeing your mind is only the beginning of this hard process. That's why we need God in every phase because, without Him and others who can help you cling to Him, we will fail every time. We are not able to defeat the darkness alone, but with God, WE CAN!

The next step is to discipline your body. Science tells us it takes forty days to break a chemical addiction. So you have forty rough, hard days ahead of you. If you listened to me and got rid of the stuff right away, then you already are ahead of the curve. You already have numbered days behind you. Par for the course is for you to stay on the path that you're on. The darkness is going to amp up his pressures here. He is going to rev up his engine and really start to scream at you. He is going to use that chemical addiction that your body has become accustomed to against you. If you are like Sammie and screens have become your problem, there is still a chemical addiction working against you. When you become addicted to something your brain starts to create extra doses of dopamine to flow through your brain. Heightening levels and feelings of happiness. Tricking your mind into thinking this "addiction" is the source of your joy. Your body starts to function with higher levels of dopamine in your system and the addiction begins.

Even a healthy person who is in great shape and has no health issues can become addicted to exercise. When the dopamine levels are faked into thinking you're happy, the body follows the brain. The brain says you need more dopamine, which in your mind means you need more of those things. When in reality, your mind just needs more dopamine. After a while, your body will be used to that dopamine level and it will need more dopamine to stimulate the brain to think it has achieved fake happiness. So it needs you to smoke more, drink more, have sex more, and do drugs more for you to break that reached dopamine level. It's a never-ending cycle that ultimately will lead to death.

That's why God says all sin will lead to death and until I learned those things about the brain, I couldn't understand God's Word in fullness. (Romans 6:23) There are so many things on this earth that can fake pure happiness. Chemicals, drugs, plants, people, feelings...I could go on, but I think you get the point. That's why God tells us when we are born again we have to let the things of this world go. He truly means we have to let it go because it will hurt us. Even kill us in some cases. There is only one form of pure true joy and that is the joy we get from having a relationship with God because our bodies cannot become addicted to Him. Our peace comes from Him. Our joy comes from Him. If we can discipline our minds, bodies, and souls to need Him, then we will be free from our Earthly addictions.

In everything that God wants from us, He wants us to be free. Because in our freedom we can find real joy again. We can find truth in Him again. We can walk with Him again in the garden and talk about the goodness of the things in all the Earth. God wants to help us overcome our self-doubt, our disobedience, and our fears. He wants us to be disciplined in Him so we can learn to surrender it all to Him for His Glory. He can never bring us into His Greatness and Glory on this Earth if we can't learn to surrender everything we are to Him. Like Sammie, we have to break the bondages of addictions to sin and death off of us and learn to walk in God in our newly found freedoms. Because when we surrender to Him, we are made whole again. Showing others that God is the Way. The Truth. The Light. That real joy does exist.

Chapter Five: Surrender

5

That was where my vision began. It began with David's surrender. As he slowly bent down to the ground, he exhaled a long deep breath. I surrender, he said to God. He picked up the stone that represented his self-doubt. I give it to you, Lord. He bent back over to pick up the next stone—his obedience. Lord, I give it to you and he exhaled. He bent back over as the sweat from his brow fell to the dusty battlefield ground. He picks up another stone. All his fears. I surrender them to you. The wind softly carried his fear away. He bent back over and picked up the fourth stone. Lord, I thank you for my discipline. For you taught me to be stronger than the darkness. You taught me to be stronger than the evil.

The sunlight shone down on his face. He stood there in the sun looking across the battlefield to an army of Philistines. An army that was brought for one purpose and one purpose alone. To destroy the Living God. David bent over and he surrendered all that he was to God. These giants will not overcome God's Army. Not today! With that last stone that he picked up, God's Lessons came and fortified his muscle memory.

* * *

You see, God is training you for your big day just like He did with David. A day when you can show the darkness everything that God has taught you about being victorious. Every lesson that David was taught up to now was reflected in his stance on that battlefield. When he came face to face with Goliath, he had not come unprepared. God had been training him to defeat his enemy. The same way God has been training you, Have you been listening? Have you been journaling? Have you been taking notes of all that your teacher has said? Because there will one day be a test that will take you out of your comfort zone and put you straight in the firing zone. Will you be ready for that day when it comes? When the enemy on the other side of the battlefield starts taunting you and saying hurtful degrading things, will you be ready to run in and shut him down? Will you be ready to hear God speak and to heed His Guidance? Will your muscles be able to remember how to effectively harness the power of speed your slingshot will need? Will you be ready to pick up your enemy's sword and cut off his head with it? Will you be ready to tell your king with confidence that God was with you and would not let these Philistines overcome the army of God?

Is your walk with God powerful enough to change generations of family after your life? Listen to the story I found in the scriptures about Hannah. (1 Samuel 1:1) Elkanah was a believer and he had two wives. Hannah, who had no children but whom he loved dearly, and Peninnah who had many children. Every year Elkanah would take his family and his offerings to Shiloh to make his sacrifice to the Lord. The priest who would receive his offerings was a man by the name of Eli. When they would get there Hannah would go to the sanctuary and she would cry and beg the Lord to bless her with a child. She would cry out inconsolably and Eli thought she was drunk with wine. He ordered her to sober up and go home, but she begged him not to think she was a bad woman. She explained that she was upset and was begging for the Lord to give her a son. He feels bad for her and blesses her. He tells her that he prays that the God of Israel will do as she asks of Him. She leaves to go home with her family. Only to know that she would return home and Peninnah would make fun of her for being without a child. Elkanah loved her that night and God made His Preparations to answer her prayers.

Later that year, Hannah gives birth to a son and she names him Samuel, which means the Lord gives. That same year Elkanah starts to prepare his family to make their trip to Shiloh for the sacrifice, but Hannah says she cannot go. When Elkanah asks her why, she tells him that she vowed to give her son to the Lord if He answered her prayers for a son. Elkanah understands that she is still breastfeeding their son and is not ready to be weaned away from her. So he tells her to stay home and take care of their son and that when he is ready they will return to Shiloh to give him to the church. Elkanah and Hannah do as they told the Lord that they would do and give him to the Lord, to the church to live a life of holy discipline.

If you will remember, it was Samuel who was the prophet who anointed David to be king! Through his mother's surrender to the Lord for a son, David was into his calling. Our surrender to the Lord richly affects the lives of those around us! I don't know about you, but I cannot wait to spend a day in the library of Heaven's Books and learn about how all of our lives are intertwined by God's goodness! When we aren't in His Throne Room, singing His Praises we'll be in the break room learning how we each came to know God and who we know that also brought others to God.

Can you only imagine how our obedience has brought others to the Lord? When we surrender our fears, doubts, anxieties, and troubles at God's Feet, He is then permitted to move mountains in the spiritual realms for us. There are so many lives that have been brought to their knees in scripture because they could not do what God can do. On their knees, they surrender and learn to trust God with everything they have. Because when we surrender our minds, will, and emotions to Him, we see His Goodness move. Like Noah surrendered himself to God and was taught to build the ark that saved his family. Abram surrendered and moved away from his family and became Abraham, the father of many generations.

Why do we wait till we cannot see any other way to move that we step out of the way and get on our knees to pray to God? It's like we are the kid on the dodgeball court who doesn't learn they have to keep moving to avoid being hit. We just sit there, expecting God to do everything for us. Then hit by hit, life fails us. Till we get back to the same place we were before. On our knees again asking to be saved. Oh, but wait we want it done our way, so we can be right. Or we want it done the way we see it done so that we can get the glory. Or, wait, we want it done a specific way because we can't see any good coming from any other way. We assume we know better than God...You know what they say about assuming, right?

So why do we wait till we cannot see any other way to let God in? Shouldn't we learn from this mistake and ask God if it's the right path to take before we move to begin with? Ask Him if it's safe to speak or what to say before opening our mouths. Ask God if we should buy this home before we open our wallets. Couldn't we avoid a lot of pain and heartache if we ask for guidance instead of repeatedly asking for God to save us from our troubles again? Just a thought…Why don't we sit still and do nothing? Why don't we wait for God to speak? Only the enemy will hurry us up. Hannah's self-doubt was evident by the anguish Peninnah was allowed to inflict on her. The scriptures don't tell us the reason why this was allowed, only that it was happening to her. Who knows, maybe her husband tried to get her to stop and so she only did it when they were away from him. Or maybe Hannah didn't like confrontation. Maybe she would rather take the abuse than confront her or tell her to stop. Who knows, maybe that was why her husband favored her so, because he thought she was frail. Maybe Peninnah was the first wife and in the family hierarchy she wore the crown, so to speak. Only God knows now why it was allowed, but it in turn it pushed Hannah closer to God.

Hannah's obedience was her faithfulness to her family and her God. I am quite sure that there was the temptation to not wait on God for the son Elkanah could provide to her. Even in the scriptures, there have been times when someone got tired of waiting on God for a son. Married to one person who was unable to give them what they wanted, so they went to a maid or another woman for the child. Abram is the testimony I am speaking of. Abram wanted a son so badly and he could not get one with his wife Sarai. Sarai was upset that she could not give Abram any sons, so she told Abram to go to Hagar, her servant, and let her build their family. Abram grew impatient and listened to her instead of seeking God's advice or permission to do so. Abrams's impatience brought him a son who upset the Godly order of Sarai's household. Ishmael was not favored by God.

Ten years after that, God spoke to Abram and told him

that He wanted to enter into a covenant with Abram. For God was going to make him the father of many nations. God told Abram that he was no longer to go by that name, but he would be called Abraham from now on. Sarai, his wife, was going to finally be given children and she would be the mother to many nations. Their son Isaac would be blessed and favored. Through his sons, he would bring forth the twelve tribes of Judah. With this great blessing came a covenant and a special requirement of all who called themselves Abraham's House. His slaves, servants, sons of their servants, children, and grandchildren had to become circumcised from here on out to show that they were descendants of Abraham.

Through the seed that Abram gave Hagar came Ishmael and the twelve Arab tribes. The Ishmaelites are where the Quran and Islamic/Muslim faiths are derived from. The Bible does not speak about Ishmael much and it does not tell us about their faith. Only God tells us that Ishmael had one daughter and twelve sons who were Arab princes. The Bible tells us that God would bless Ishmael and his tribe would be many but they would not be the inheritors of God's Kingdom like Abraham's son, Isaac. His people lived in the Arabian Peninsula and were great traders/ barters. When Ishmael was fourteen years old, Abraham and Sarah had Issac. Abraham was one hundred years old when Issac was born. However, Abraham sent Ishmael and Hagar away after that. Abraham was deeply saddened by Sarah's demand to make his firstborn son and wife leave. However, God calmed him down and said that because Ishmael was his firstborn, God would make his descendants a great nation as well. Hagar and Ishmael wandered through the Desert of Paran until they were out of food and water. Both of them were crying to the Lord. An angel came from the Lord and told her not to worry that God was with them and would take care of them. He opened her eyes and gave her a well to drink from. Ishmael grew up and got married to an Egyptian woman.

What would have happened to the bloodlines if Abraham had waited on God instead of allowing Sarai's impatience and disappointments to pursuede his decisions? I feel that I would be misleading you if I didn't tell you about all the research I have uncovered to write this book. I feel that I have been given a glimpse into history and I now have a greater sense of purpose and a will given through this research. I have uncovered parts of the information for you, but to unfold everything before you would not do it justice. I have walked through the lives of over 50 men and women in and around history in the family bloodlines from Noah to Jesus Christ. You would not believe the clever orchestration that was required to bring these lives from deep in the mud out into God's Glory. Looking up their family trees was just the beginning of the unraveling of the greatness of God.

Every testimony of these lives is riddled with disobedience, sin, murder, abuse, lies, deception, unfaithfulness, fear, mayhem, jealousy, idolatry...I could go on. But the fact of the matter remains...that God was glorified in the end. Every life was full of so many mistakes and misfortune, yet in every situation, they were brought to their knees and had to surrender to God's Will. Every one of them. Don't you see? God loves you so much, that He will not leave you in that mess you have made. He is still there saying, "Hey, My Beloved, Take My Hand and let Me help you up."

He doesn't need to know what those people did to you, He already knows it all. He said, "The vengeance is Mine." He doesn't need to know what you did, He saw it all. He is

135

omnipresent. He doesn't need to know what they said, He hears all things. He doesn't need to know how bad they hurt you, He collects every tear. The thing about surrender is that when you are in that place where you can't do anything else and you are out of options on which way to go, that is when God can do great things.

That's where I was when I went in for my eye surgery. My heart was so bad that they weren't sure that I would make it through the surgery. But God did. My eyes were so blurry and not working because of my heart and circulation that they weren't sure that the eye surgery would work. But God did. I wasn't sure which voice I wanted to listen to. I just knew I needed my eyes to work to take care of my daughter. But God did. I wasn't sure the enemy would let me walk away from the hospital after the surgery. But God did. I wasn't sure I would ever get to see my baby again. But God did.

Through all my fears, pains, and trust issues God saw me differently on the other side of the surgery. He saw me whole again. He saw me with a healed heart. He saw me walking and testifying about all the goodness He had done. He saw me kissing my husband and eating fruit with him in the hospital room. He saw me telling these doctors I knew who healed me. That it was God. He saw me sitting in front of my church testifying that God did a great thing in me. He saw me glorifying HIM! Because nothing could be done by the doctors, by my husband, by my family. I was dying and there was nothing we could do about it. My heart was broken. BUT GOD!

So let me ask you this... What are you waiting for? Sick and tired of the life that you were dealt with? Then do it God's Way. Having trouble with coworkers and misfits at work? Then do it God's Way. Feeling depressed and sick of life? Then do it God's Way. Tired of seeing our country abused and mistreated? Then elect Godly men and women who do things God's Way. Tired of seeing your children taught unGodly principles and morals? Then get them to a school that is run by Christians. Are you getting what I am laying down here? If you want to see changes then you have to be willing to make the changes required! If you want your life to remain the same then do nothing. But if you want to see God move in a mighty way through your life then you need to move towards God. (James 4:8)

If you have already read the first four chapters and you have put those words into effect in your life, then you have already seen God begin to work and do amazing things. I can only imagine the testimony that you are giving to others about overcoming your self-doubt and what God has done in your mind. Now that you see yourself the way that HE sees you. Oh mercy, I wish I could hear your story about learning to obey Him. I wonder how He has moved into your church and your family now that you're obediently seeking His Face and reading His Words daily.

Oh Hallelujah! You're going to have to get in touch with my Facebook page and tell me how you and God overcame the fear that was in your way! I literally want to hear how you kicked satan in the tailbone out of your house! You see how excited I get, knowing that the goodness of God is already moving the mountains that are in your way? I imagine that was how David felt as he walked into King Saul's tent that day, He walked in giggling and clapping his hands because He wanted to know how King Saul was going to handle God's Business. For David had his own testimonies that had him excited. He walked into camp, giddy that he was in the presence of God's Great Army only to see them cowering in the corner scared to death.

He had to have been walking around with a tone of disappointment in his voice. Looking for a brother in arms to stand up with him and to rally these men to stand up and fight for the ONE TRUE LIVING GOD! Can you believe this uncircumcised Philistine?!? Are you going to stand there and let this bully push you around? You are a soldier of the Almighty! Stand up! Stand up!!! So He was summoned to King Saul's tent because the king needed to be calmed down with the lyre again. Only this time he got warrior David. He didn't get sweet little guitar-playing David. He got furious David. He got there is a lion threatening my herd David. He got there is a bear with my sheep in his mouth David.

He got, "I have a slingshot and a Loving God on my side!" kind of David that was not going to let this evil walk up into his house and take his brothers away from him. He didn't know what was wrong with the army that day, but he was prepared for what he was called to do. He had already prepared himself to be ready for war. He had already practiced his skills to defend himself. He had already spent time with God in his secret place to ward off all evil from his path. He was already anointed for the place God called him to be. He had already worshiped before the Lord and God found him worthy. You see, everything David had in him was laid at the feet of God to do His Will. He was surrendered to God.

That day when David was bending over and picking up his stones to use against Goliath, he was surrendering all his power, strength, and training to God. He was willing to give his life to defend God's Honor. When you have given everything to God and you have submitted yourself to do God's Will, then you surrender your wishes for your life. You let go of your dreams because they are no longer important to you. You surrender your wants because they are no longer valuable to your eyes. You surrender your journey because it no longer matters what you will face because you know God is with you. You surrender your belongings and possessions because they no longer are yours. You gave them to God to use. You surrender your all to Him. He takes all your fears, trust issues, doubts, failures, anger, pain, hurt, rage, addictions, and problems. He takes them all and He turns them into dust.

When you can get to the place where you give everything to Him, that is when you will see God move in a mighty way. That is when you will see your body healed. That is when you will see your children return home to you. That is when you will hear and see Heaven move on Earth. Because when God is allowed to reign victorious over your problems, then the darkness has no hold on your life any longer. You will then possess the power to change lives in your testimony. You will be able to talk with mean coworkers and bring them to a harmonious place. That is when you can walk in who God has called you to be; His Ambassador.

You will no longer be held by the things that kept you bound in fear and anger. The anxieties that kept you from making friends are no longer there. You will be able to walk in confidence and power. Not in the way that others walk, but in the way that the time you spent with God has trained you to walk. Just like David, you will be able to walk into the king's tent and ask him to go out on that battlefield to slay the enemy of the Lord his God. That is when the scripture in the Bible comes to fruition in your walk with God.

"If God is for you, then who can be against you?" Romans 8:31

I used to read that scripture with no experience of what it

truly meant. When I was young, I could only understand things the way a baby does. Simply and with more questions than I had answers. But then as I grew up to be a little older, I read it differently. I would think of it like this. That yes, many things could come against you, if you were a follower of Christ. Because if you remember I was walking with God and the darkness hated it. So he would attack. I was in a constant state of defense. I couldn't breathe because the smoke of the battlefield arrows would never cease firing. Then now, as I read it after my healing, I remember my thoughts before my surgery. Lord, I surrender to Your Will. Lord, if you heal me on this operating table then let it be done. If you see it is my time to come home to you, let it be done. You see, if you surrender yourself to His Will then it doesn't matter what could be done to you. Because it is in His Hands.

If the darkness made its way into my operating room, then it was God's Will. If the doctor submitted to the Lord, as I asked him to, then it was God's Will. If the nurse's eyes were open and she was there to take care of me, then it was God who deemed it so. You see nothing happens in our lives if God doesn't permit it. Even unto our death, because nothing happens without His Permission. He tells us in scripture that we are a slave to something. We can surrender our life to God and be righteous on the day of His Coming. Or we can surrender to the evil around us and let it kill us. If we are a slave to something, let it be to God who gives us eternal life after death. Let it be to a life with a purpose to choose good over evil. Let us build others up instead of tearing them down. Let us bring others to the Lord and teach them to be disciples as well.

~ * ~

* * *

Just because God has brought us through these battles, doesn't mean the enemy won't try to use these same tactics against us again. Remember God says in scripture that the enemy is a lion who seeks continuously to devour us however he can. If he sees that having a co-worker to attack your integrity gets you thrown off your path. Then he will use another co-worker to attack your honor and honesty this time. If he knows that attacking your children or your grandchildren will get you to fly off the deep end and start acting unGodly, then he will constantly use them against you. If you can't make it to church to be refilled because your health is keeping you away, then your health will always be under attack.

This was a hard lesson for me to learn. But when you have been attacked as many times as I have been attacked by the enemy you start to see a pattern. Once God shows you those patterns, then you can never unsee them. They are always there. If you start dispelling them and the effects the attacks have on you, then the enemy gets even more upset. Let me give you some helpful advice. JOURNAL! JOURNAL! JOURNAL! Because after a while you will start seeing a replication of evil that comes against you, and when you see that you need to write it down. Make it known to your memory. Make it known to history. Because if the enemy has used it to attack you, then you can guarantee he has done it to another hundred aside from you! You need to know how you defeated it. You need to remember how God took it away from you. You need to know what to tell your children you did when you had the same problem they are having when they come to you for your help.

It was the same with David after he became king. He defeated the Philistines and Goliath that day. But if you read on in scripture you read that David had to defeat them over and over again. The enemy kept using the Philistines to attack God's People. So like David, we have to be prepared for another attack. It may be the same but it may also change completely. When you're dealing with satan, you can never be sure when and where an attack is coming from. That is why it is so important to be in your Word and talk with God all the time. The scriptures are a valuable tool in knowing what an attack looks like. Partnered with the Holy Spirit you can never go wrong. No matter how deceiving he wants to be. He will fail. The darkness will always lose when he comes at you.

That is why I cannot stress to you enough the importance of memorizing scriptures as they are written. My ex had a restraining order placed against me because when I found out that he was cheating on me with another woman I made a very bad phone call threatening his life. Listen, I was very upset and depressed because of the bad marriage I was in. It's not an excuse because you shouldn't call someone up and threaten their life, no matter what they have done. Because only God knew that he was going to get more evil as time went long. But let's just say that in my experience if something feels off about a person or their family when you're dating, do yourself a favor and cut it off before you get married. After two years, he filed that I had broken the restraining order probation by giving him a Valentine's Day card...Yes, you can laugh. I am laughing with you. Sigh!

Nonetheless, his lawyer made the argument that if the magistrate was wrong and I was some sort of psychopath out to kill him it would be on them if they didn't have me picked up. So over the Thanksgiving Holiday, I sat in jail waiting on a bond hearing. It took the judge sixteen hard days to get me the hearing and once it took place, I was out.

We can say it was many sorts of things. That any number of people should have been held accountable and be sued but in my heart, I knew I was being punished by God. There is nothing anyone can say that could tell me that God didn't put me in that jail cell to learn a lesson.

In the back of the police car on the way in as I was crying my head off, the police officer tried to help me prepare for what was to come. He knew the charges were crap and that it was an abuse of the courts, so he tried to prepare me. It's now a big blur and I don't remember what he said to me. But I do remember what God said to me on the way there. When I was crying and the tears fell down my face, I asked God why he was allowing my ex to do these horrible things to me. I'll never forget what He said to me.

"You have to learn to listen to Me and My Voice. You have to know you can't follow the world. You have to follow me now."

Once the check-in procedures were complete and I was placed in my cell, I sat down on my cot and rolled up in the cheap blanket they provided. I cried myself to sleep. I had a cellmate. I don't know that I ever got her name. I only had a few conversations with her and the first one was asking her if she knew how I could get a hold of a Bible. She laughed and said I could ask the guards. If I was lucky someone might give me one if I gave them something else…This was a local jail not even a prison. Who knows if she was telling the truth or not but I already wanted to vomit. But I left the cell and we had an open common area with a TV that we could watch. So I went out there away from her and sat at the tables and pretended to be watching TV as I thought to myself.

Of course, during these times the guards did walkthroughs. My guess was to keep order and the peace, but that was when I realized I knew all my guards personally. So I asked one of my friends if they could get me a Bible. The next few days were very hard on me because I really didn't know anyone in there to talk to. I was cut off from the outside world and didn't know how to do anything from there to help myself or my family who hopefully was trying to get me out. The only scriptures that I could recite were the ones that I had memorized and even then they didn't help me much. I recited them over and over in my head to draw closer to God. I would talk to Him and after the first day, I knew what I had to do. I asked someone if I could get a piece of paper and pencil to write with and I wrote down what God told me I had to do. After He gave me the list of things to do the Holy Spirit left the impression on my heart that I would not get out until I completed the tasks. So it was on me to be obedient and surrender to His Will.

I was terrified. It was only three things but those three things were impossible in the position I was put in. How was God expecting me to get these three things done in jail with nothing but hardened women who hated people like me? They were intimidating and scary to me. As I sat by myself, I began to build my strength up to get just one done. The first one, so I thought, was pretty easy. There were only a few channels on the TV and one of them played a video broadcast of Dr. Charles Stanley. He was a minister with a home church in Atlanta, GA. I listened to his podcasts at home on the occasion. God told me I had to get up at 7 every morning and go out to the TV and watch Dr. Stanley's program. Simple enough, right? What harm could happen by quietly listening to a little TV show while everyone was still sleeping? The first morning, I got the courage to go out there. Because I was diabetic they came every morning at 6:30 AM to take me to the nurse to test my blood sugars and get my insulin shot. So I had the wake-up call taken care of.

I got up and took care of my diabetes, then I would come back and turn on the TV to watch the show. It was up on the wall, so the guard put me in the common room and I went and sat down. I looked up at the TV and it hit me...I can't reach the controls to turn the TV on! What do I do now? Crap! I looked to see if there was a guard to ask for help but it was quiet and no one was around. Well as I looked around I thought to myself, the table here was set in the concrete, it wouldn't move. If I stand up on the table, I could cut it on. So I climbed up on the table and I was still too short to reach the controls. One of the other cellmates saw me having these problems and came out of her cell. I quickly apologized for waking her and began to sit down to tell her I was just trying to watch the pastor on the TV before everyone got up.

Her face didn't change. She climbed on the table and cut on the TV to the program I wanted got down off the table and nodded her head at me. She never smiled, asked me my name, or acknowledged my thank you. She just turned around and went back to her cell. She was a lot taller than me and a pretty stout woman. I remember thinking to myself, "I hope she never wants to fight me because she'd hurt me pretty bad." I prayed that never happened. I sat down at the table right below the TV and quietly listened to Dr. Stanley. I felt like I had just accomplished a space mission to Mars. God gave me a task and I was doing it. The first item on His List was done! Check! Or was it?

The next thing I know I start hearing screaming and yelling like a demon was attacking an individual in the farthest cell from me. The moment I heard it scream my head shot around to see where it was coming from. I thought I was in a horror movie of some sort. The next thing I knew people started to get angry and started yelling at others to shut up and go back to sleep. People started to come out of their cells and were looking to get into a fight. I remember hearing amongst the chaos, God's Voice muted the cell mates screaming and I heard Him say,

"Turn back around and watch the TV. Do not turn around. Keep your eyes on me."

I listened immediately. The first voice that was screaming like a demon started to speak in a language I could understand. She began screaming as she came out of her cell and told me to cut the TV off. There were a lot of bad words and I'll spare you reading those. But the moment was intense. There she and her cellmate were outside their cell screaming at me. But I had to listen to God. I looked up and I felt like I was shaking. I heard her scream really loud as she took off running across the cell common area. The next thing I knew there was a scuffle of thumps and punches thrown. I heard them land their punch. Then some guards came in and took the two girls away. The guard ordered everyone to calm down or they would make us get back in our cells. Everyone listened and I took a deep breath.

A few of the other women came and sat down with me and asked if I was okay. I explained that after she started screaming at me, God told me to look at the screen and not turn around. I told them He promised me that I would be okay, but I didn't know what had happened because I listened to Him. They began to explain to me who those two girls were and what had happened. Apparently, they were being transferred to prison because they were convicted of murdering their boyfriends in cold blood. They had stabbed them in a ritual. A couple of the women said they thought she was possessed by the way she ran across the floor with the shive. I asked them who stopped her. Because I heard the fighting going on. They said that one of the other cellmates and a few of her friends stood up and stood between the girls and me. But there was no fighting that happened. Not that they could see.

However, I know, even as I sit here today that heavy punches were thrown and several large bodies hit the floor. I know the sounds that I heard with my ears and the only conclusion that I can come to is that what I was hearing was not in the physical. But in the spiritual plane. I was hearing demons hit the floor. I was hearing evil being defeated on my behalf. I was hearing God's Heavy Weights standing between me and my soul. Because when it was over I turned around and there were no bodies on the floor. I was only witnessing two women being dragged out to other confinements till they left our facility. Because I never saw them ever again.

I would NEVER tell anyone, regardless of the strength of their faith to put themselves knowingly in danger. I look back and even though the task wasn't something crazy like standing up to a drug dealer or confronting a murderer, I still feel like I have to say that God has to be in it 100% or you're just asking for trouble. Because you can never assume to know where the darkness will come from. You have to know that God put you there and that HE will have your back. He only asked me to watch TV and read my Bible. But evil sprung up from a source I wasn't expecting. To be honest, I wasn't even expecting trouble. I thought it was a lesson to learn about obeying Him, no matter what others said. I thought that maybe I would get spit on or maybe cussed. But to say I was attacked by a woman who was possessed by evil with a toothbrush shank?!? How could I have thought that would happen? So make sure that you are hearing straight from God to do something and that you are listening to His every detail because if you mess up it could cost you your life.

It was a few days later and I don't know where or when it came but when I went back to my cell one day to go to the bathroom there was the Bible I had asked for sitting on my bed for me. I was then prepared to do my next task on God's list. There was a young lady that God wanted me to witness to and bring her to the Lord. Up unto that moment in my life, I had only witnessed to one other individual about the goodness of God and His Grace and it was someone I knew personally. I had never met this girl before and I knew nothing about her, her family, or her situation. But God wanted me to tell her about God and ask her if she wanted to accept Jesus as her Lord and Savior.

I was nervous and I felt like I didn't know how to effectively answer any questions that she might have about God. I didn't study Biblical Theology or have my masters in bringing others into a more intimate relationship with God. All I knew was what I had read in the Bible up to now and the things God had shown me in my private time with Him. But it was the second thing on my list and I had to get it done. So one day I went and sat at her table outside her cell and waited till she came out to talk to her.

We had a nice conversation and I encouraged her to go to a couple of churches that I knew of to continue her walk with God. I felt a sense of urgency for her to get to know the Lord and I didn't know why till a month or so later. She was still there when I left jail and a few weeks after I got out I tried to find out what had happened to her. After she got out, she started back into the same lifestyle of drinking and drugs. She was driving home late one night after partying, lost control of her car, and died in a car accident. I still pray to this day that she was real in her time with me about asking God to come into her heart. But I won't know for sure until I get to Heaven and see His Face to ask Him where she is.

I was then left with my third task and I will admit, this one was hard because of my stance on life choices at the time. Then I believed that your life was your own and it was none of my business where you found love. As long as I didn't have to see it, to each his/her own. The Holy Spirit told me that this girl was a lesbian and that God wanted me to give her a booklet on the matter. I felt that God wanted me to talk to her about it and see if she would open up to me about it. I was scared to death because this was the same woman who helped me turn the TV on and who stood up against the girls for me. So one day she was sitting alone at one of the tables and I felt God nudge me to talk to her about it.

So I walked over and asked her if I could sit down. I had the discussion that I needed to have with her and the moment we got done and I walked back to my cell to breathe a sigh of relief, the officer came across the monitor and told me to get my stuff together. I was getting out. I mean it was literally seconds later after I finished my list God had already made preparations for me to go home. I had never experienced God like that in my entire life. Seeing Him work and provide for me when I had lost all control of everything in my life. It may be too much information but I started my period a couple of days after I got there and God made a way for me to get the things needed to handle my business. Only God could have known that I would need those items and orchestrated providing them to me without help from any other cellmates.

That's why I know that obeying Him is vital to our existence as active Christians because there is evil lurking around every corner and if we are not careful to abide by His

Commands we could find ourselves in great danger. A danger in the physical and spiritual realms. We have to be sure to meditate on His Word carefully day and night. We have to be in church absorbing and practicing His Instructions so that we can be ready if we are ever in a position like that again. I have made it my mission to write and journal everything I learn. So that generations of people who come after me can step up when God says it's time and become the warrior on the wall in my place. I may not be here forever, but I want what I have learned to be my legacy for all those who came after me to follow in my footsteps and take up their shields.

I do not sin, because it takes me away from God. I do not drink because it dulls my senses against the darkness. I do not use or do drugs because it alters my brain chemistry and I cannot act or hear God the way I need to to protect myself or others around me if the evil would come again. I carry my anointing oil and God's Word with me so that if I have someone in my path who needs help, prayers, or deliverance from evil I am there ready to remove it from their life through Jesus' Name. I rest in God because He is faithful and true. I fast to draw nearer to Him and to beg for His Attention. I stay in prayer continuously so that I can always know what His Voice sounds like and not be tricked by evil into thinking it can speak in God's Place to fool me.

You see, even though satan hates God with everything he has he still knows God and His Goodness. The devil knows how and who God is to us. He used to be one of God's trusted angels in Heaven until he was cast away from Him. So he knows how to manipulate God's Word to distort and manipulate lies to look like the truth. He knows how to trick and fool you into believing something is real when it is not. He has mastered the art of terrifying, scaring, lying, and causing fear in everyday activities. He is the father of all lies and the master of evil in every way. He is not to be messed with and he has no equal. He wants it that way. If you think "selling your soul" to him will make you the best evil has to offer, then he has tricked you into believing another lie. Because he is the only master of evil and he will not share the throne with anyone else. Including you. Especially you. So don't be fooled by a fallen angel doomed to destruction and hell when you can have a life free and happy in God's Kingdom here on Earth and in Heaven after we die.

Make no mistake here in my writings. Our enemy is not with others, even people who are not saved. Our war is with the devil and the principalities of darkness that serve evil. It is not against other humans who have not found their faith in God yet. Those are people we need to be in prayer for. Those are the people we need to intercede and fast for. But my friends, remember, no matter how ugly they get your job is to be God's Grace, Mercy, Love, and Joy too. If they are all consumed with evil and it is more for you to bear then walk away from them. Do not put yourself in danger and don't get into fights with them. Not in the physical or digital. I see too many instances where Christians want to be right so badly that they ruin any bridge they might have with an unsaved individual because they would rather be right than show God's Love. If you ever find yourself in that mindset then you need to pull back and spend some time with God because you are falsely representing His Heart for them.

God would never want you to lash out at an unbeliever to push them further away from Him. Our duty is to reflect Christ and to stand between them and the harm that evil could bring to them. That means you give them your coat when they are cold. You feed them when you see they are hungry. You wash their feet and give them a place to rest when they are broken and weak. That is who God has called us all to be to the lost and those who have been lied to. Christians are the ones who pull others out of the darkness and bring them back into God's Light. I would say that as a Christian, my days get more discouraged every time I look at the political arena.

On either side, they both have taken some pretty ugly unGodly stances that have disappointed my walk with Christ and my hope for humanity. I see more Christians slinging mud than I see saving the lost. It's almost like Christians are standing over the pit asking what president they voted for before throwing them a rope to get out of the pit they were in. Like we are only called to save the already saved. But my friends, that was not who we are called to be. We are called to save the lost and forgotten. We are called to share the good news with everyone we meet. We are called to bring honor, glory, and hope to the ones who have lost their way and bring them back into the fold to find their Savior again.

How can we expect to save anyone who doesn't see the good in us? Why would we want anyone to be like us if we are only displaying bad attributes? If they only see condemnation and unforgiveness then how could we expect for them to overcome those areas in their life? We need to show them that Christ showed us a better way to handle the stresses of this day. That we don't need to run to alcohol like our uncles did. That we don't need to have a sexual release valve to overcome our confidence problems. We don't need a bottle of wine to relax. Or that we don't need to get away from our kids to have fun. That we don't need to follow the ways that the world has come up with to get through this life.

That's when we surrender to obeying God and the ways He wants us to live. It is only then that we can have hope, joy, faithfulness in our relationships, gentleness in our speech and actions, peace in our spirits, and true happiness in our souls. Because in Him we have all the steps we need to glorify Him for all He is doing for us. For all that He continually is doing for us. The closer we can get to Him the more we can do effectively. In our relationships to lift Him up and glorify Him. In our stances, we can show others how to reflect Him better. In our voice, we can show them how to sing His Praises in our Spirit and in our Truth like He has asked of us.

In our anger, to show them we are righteous and can lift God up the right way. Even when we are afraid we, can be strong. In our pain, we can still love. In our sorrow, we can still lift our countenance. In our hurt, we can still be fruitful. In all our ways we can acknowledge Him and He will direct our paths.

So that when we are victorious we can maintain our honor because we know where it came from and who taught it to us to hold onto. It was God who taught David all he was able to do. Everything from preparing his mind, body, and soul to overcome Goliath but also in what to do next. I pray that when you are standing in your castle balcony your righteousness will carry you into a place of greater honor and bring God more glory than any of us could have ever imagined.

That the attacks from the darkness will always be a threat to you and that you will always be prepared for them to come. I think that David had gotten comfortable in his high-rise castle overlooking the Israelites. Because one can get too comfortable sitting next to God in the high places. You can begin to think that you are no longer able to be attacked. You have pushed yourself into a place where no one can ever hurt you again and you begin to get comfortable with the place that God put you. Because when we read more in scripture we see that God wasn't done teaching David about the many flaws of a man.

Or maybe not so much that there were more flaws in a man as much as there were more temptations from the darkness. We see and read about David's intimate desires that his private time took him. On that balcony that day that he first saw Bathsheba, David's honor should have taken him to another place in his castle away from her. But he did not do the honorable thing and stayed away from her. He kept going back and fed the lust that was building in his heart. When he should have removed the hold the temptation had on him by moving himself further away from her. I'm sure David's castle had many rooms in it. I am sure he could have said I don't want to have my room in the west wing any longer. Please move my bedroom and all my things to the East side of the villa.

David should have learned from his ancestor's mistakes. Lord, knows the mistake had been made at least three times in his family bloodline. First in Judah with the lust after his wife passed away to fill the needs of his flesh. Then Abraham with Hagar to have a son. Then in his father, Jesse with the desire for his wife's servant. You see, he had many lives he could have learned this lesson from. He was single, in the same space that Judah was in. He didn't have a wife to fulfill his fleshly desires and needed it fixed. He wanted, just like Abraham. He wanted a wife who could give him a son. He wanted to build a family. He lusted in his flesh like his father and wanted someone he couldn't have. She was not his to take.

Instead of going to God for his answers, he turned away

from God and followed his flesh. I am king. I can order her to my bed. I can have anyone I want. Instead of giving God the chance to provide for him in God's Timing, he rushed in and took her for himself. Instead of asking God to give him a Godly-approved woman, he took Bathsheba from her husband and had him killed by sending him to the front lines of battle and making sure he was killed. He couldn't bear the weight of sin that he had brought on his life and instead of going to God to repent and put an end to the sin, David gets her pregnant in the sin before cleansing his soul of the harm he had caused.

Citations:

(Cit. 1)

The Mysterious Childhood of King David
Author: Ushi
Date: November 18, 2018
https://www.anumuseum.org.il/blog